MFK FISHER

How to Cook a Wolf

NORTH POINT PRESS
San Francisco 1988

North Point Press
850 Talbot Avenue
Berkeley, California
94706

For Lawrence Paul

Contents

Introduction to the
Revised Edition

How to Cook a Wolf was first published in 1942, when war-time shortages were at their worst. It was revised by the author in 1951, by the addition of copious marginal notes and footnotes and a special section of additional recipes. These have now been incorporated in their proper places in the text, and are enclosed in brackets, as is, for an example, the Introduction to the Revised Edition that follows.

THE EDITORS

[It is hard to know whether war or peace makes the greater changes in our vocabularies, both of the tongue and of the spirit.

Certain it is, however, that in less than ten years this book about living as decently as possible with the ration cards and blackouts and like miseries of World War II has assumed some of the characteristics of quaintness. It has become, in short, in so short a time, a kind of period piece. In its own way it is as curious, as odd, as any fat old gold-ribbed volume called, a hundred years ago instead of nine or ten, *Ladies' Indispensable Assis-*

tant and Companion, One of the Best Systems of Cookery Ever Published for Sister, Mother, and Wife. . . .

Of course, it is difficult, in spite of the obvious changes in our physical problems since *How to Cook a Wolf* was first published in 1942, to say truthfully and exactly when we are at war.

Now we are free of ration cards (It was shocking, the other day, to hear that after almost twelve years gas rationing had come to an end in England. What a long time! Too long. . .): no more blue and red tokens, no more flimsy stamps to tear out or not tear out.

We can buy as much porterhouse and bourbon and powdered sugar as our purses will allow, given the rise of almost one hundred percent in the cost of such gastronomical amenities.

We need not worry, temporarily at least, about basic cupboards for blackouts . . . while at the same time we try not to think, even superficially, about what and when and how and where to nourish survivors of the next kind of bomb.

Thus stated, the case for Peace is feeble.

One less chilling aspect of the case for War II is that while it was still a shooting affair it taught us survivors a great deal about daily living that is valuable to us now that it is, ethically at least, a question of cold weapons and hot words. (In one week from the writing of this cautious statement, or one hour from the final printing of it, double ridicule can be its lot. Are weapons ever cold?)

There are very few men and women, I suspect, who cooked and marketed their way through the past war without losing forever some of the nonchalant extravagance of the twenties. They will feel, until their final days on earth, a kind of culinary caution: butter, no matter how unlimited, is a precious substance not lightly to be wasted; meats, too, and eggs, and all the far-brought spices of the world, take on a new significance, having once been so rare. And that is good, for there can be no more shameful carelessness than with the food we eat for life itself. When we exist without thought or thanksgiving we are not men, but beasts.

War is a beastly business, it is true, but one proof that we are human is our ability to learn, even from it, how better to exist. If this book, written in one wartime, still goes on helping to solve that unavoidable problem, it is worth reading again, I think, no matter what its quaint superficiality, its sometimes unintentionally grim humor.

That is why I have added to it, copiously. Not everything new in it is purely practical, of course. But even the wolf, temporarily appeased, cannot live on bread alone.

(And *that* is why I have added even more, I have sneaked other recipes into the book. Some are hopelessly extravagant— 16 eggs!—and some are useful and some are funny, and one is actually for bread that even a wolf would live on.

These "extra" recipes are culinary rules to be followed with not a thought of the budget, not even half an ear cocked toward that sniffing at the door. I know, because I *know*, that one good whiff from any of these dishes will send the beast cringing away, in a kind of extrasensory and ultra-moral embarrassment.)]

M. F. K. F.

There's a whining at the threshold,
There's a scratching at the floor.
To work! To work! In Heaven's name!
The wolf is at the door!

C. P. S. GILMAN

How to

Cook a Wolf

How to Be
Sage Without Hemlock

How often when they find a sage
As sweet as Socrates or Plato
They hand him hemlock for his wage
Or bake him like a sweet potato!
Taking the Longer View,
DON MARQUIS

In spite of all the talk and study about our next years, and all the silent ponderings about what lies within them for our sons [Why only sons? Since I wrote this I have acquired two daughters, and they too shape the pattern's pieces, and the texture of my belief!] it seems plain to us that many things are wrong in the present ones that can be, *must* be, changed. Our texture of belief has great holes in it. Our pattern lacks pieces.

One of the most obvious fallacies is that of what we should eat. Wise men forever have known that a nation lives on what its body assimilates, as well as on what its mind acquires as knowledge. Now, when the hideous necessity of the war machine takes steel and cotton and humanity, our own private personal secret mechanism must be stronger, for selfish comfort as well as for the good of the ideals we believe we believe in.

One of the stupidest things in an earnest but stupid school of culinary thought is that each of the three daily meals should be "balanced." [This still goes on in big-magazine advertising, but there seems less and less insistence on it in real life: baby-doctors and even gynecologists admit that most human bodies choose their own satisfactions, dietetically and otherwise.]

In the first place, not all people need or want three meals each day. Many of them feel better with two, or one and one-half, or five.

Next, and most important perhaps, "balance" is something that depends entirely upon the individual. One man, because of his chemical setup, may need many proteins. Another, more nervous perhaps [or even more phlegmatic], may find meats and eggs and cheeses an active poison, and have to live with what grace he can on salads and cooked squash.

Of course, where countless humans are herded together, as in military camps or schools or prisons, it is necessary to strike what is ironically called the happy medium. In this case what kills the least number with the most ease is the chosen way.

And, in most cases now, the happy medium, gastronomically, is known as the balanced diet.

A balanced diet in almost any well-meaning institution is a plan for meals that means that at each of the three daily feedings the patient is given a set amount of carbohydrates and protein and starch, and a certain amount of International Units, and a certain number of vitamins in correct ratio to the equally certain amount of minerals, and so on and so forth.

What it boils down to [an unhappy if accidental play on words: the trouble with almost all cooking is the boiling down thereof, and the resultant dearth of gastronomical guts] is that for breakfast you have fruit or a fruit juice, hot or cold cereal, eggs and cured pork in any of about four ways, bread or toast, and coffee (or tea, or milk). For the noon meal you eat soup, potato, meat, two vegetables or one and a "salad," a pudding or cake of some sort, and tea or coffee or milk. And for supper, to continue the drearily familiar song, you probably eat soup again, eggs again, a vegetable again, and stewed fruit . . . and tea, coffee, or milk.

Of course, this sad rigmarole varies a little in every institution, but it can be considered either a proof of democracy or a shocking human blindness that intrinsically it is the same at the Arizona Biltmore and your county hospital. [Of course, oysters or caviar before the soup (*consommé double*); beef filet grilled with *pâté de foies gras*, instead of eggs; a cloud-light pile of zucchini Florentine instead of the respectable peas-and-carrots of Old Watanooga . . . and *compote de fruits* instead of stewed prunes . . . and it is *still* a meal of ghastly good balance!]

One of the saving graces of the less-monied people of the world has always been, theoretically, that they were forced to eat more unadulterated, less dishonest food than the rich-bitches. It begins to look as if that were a lie. In our furious efforts to prove that all men are created equal we encourage our radios, our movies, above all our weekly and monthly magazines, to set up a fantastic ideal in the minds of family cooks, so that everywhere earnest eager women are whipping themselves and their budgets to the bone to provide three "balanced" meals a day for their men and children.

It is true, without argument of any kind, that as a people we know much more about correct human nutrition than we did even a few years ago. But we are somewhat confused by all the exciting names [riboflavin, monosodium glutamate, arsofini-barborundum . . . all fine things, when used with a modicum of nonhysteria . . .] and more so by the solemn exhortations of the "food editors" of all the slick magazines we read to improve ourselves.

We want, and not only because we are told to but because we sense instinctively that it is right, to give Mortimer III the vitamins and minerals he should absorb in order to be a fine sturdy little Mortimer indeed. But what a rat race it is: formulas, schedules, piles of dishes, little dabs of this and that three times every monotonously regular day! And Mortimer III rebels sometimes ("Poached egg *again*? I had one *yesterday*!") and sometimes so does his stomach, because how can you know that tomato juice and toast play hob together in certain insides?

This bugbear of meal-balancing is hard not only on the wills and wishes of the great American family, but is pure hell on the pocketbook. There are countless efficient-looking pages in "home magazines" each month, marked into twenty-eight or so squares with a suggested menu for each meal of the week, and then one supposedly tempting dish to prepare every day. The lead usually cries, "Let's economize, Mothers! Here is how you can do it for only 39¢ per person! Try it, and help Uncle Sam!" [Not today, you can't! Not if you follow the balanced-meal plan, you can't! Not even if you buy it wholesale and cook it for fifteen people at a time, you can't! I know. I tried it. I went to auctions for unwanted potatoes, for dented cans. . . . All I got was more red in my budget book and more gray in my hair.]

And then you start reading the familiar old routine: BREAK-FAST, fruit juice, hot or cold cereal, scrambled eggs with bacon, buttered toast, coffee or tea or milk; NOONDAY MEAL, tomato soup, beef patties, mashed potatoes, lima beans, Waldorf sal . . . but why go on? It is familiar enough.

It is disheartening, too. Now, of all times in our history, we should be using our minds as well as our hearts in order to survive . . . to live gracefully if we live at all. And people who fought to know better keep telling us to go on as our mothers did, when it should be obvious to the zaniest of us that something was wrong with that plan, gastronomically if not otherwise. [It may not have seemed wrong *then*. Now we have polio, let us admit. But fifty years ago babies died of Summer Complaint. We progress.]

No. We must change. If the people set aside to instruct us cannot help, we must do it ourselves. We must do our own balancing, according to what we have learned and also, for a change, according to what we have *thought*.

Given that Mortimer should eat fruit, vegetables, a starch, and perhaps meat or another protein every day. (Almost any good dietician will tell you that a normal "rounded" food plan includes all the necessary vitamins without recourse to pills and elixirs.) Given also that Mortimer is in average physical fitness. (Otherwise he and you should be guided by a doctor, who might tell you to stop all fruit, or even milk, for a time. . . .)

Then, instead of combining a lot of dull and sometimes actively hostile foods into one routine meal after another, three times a day and every day, year after year, in the earnest hope that you are being a good provider, try this simple plan: *Balance the day, not each meal in the day*. [This is a very solemn footnote, and if I could I would, a hundred and eight years from now and with serene confidence, make another footnote to this footnote. It is true, and true things are worth repeating, perhaps *ad nauseam* because all truth smacks of smugness, but never to the point of ridiculosity.]

Try it. It is easy, and simple, and fun, and—perhaps most important—people like it.

At first older ones who have been conditioned through many unthinking years will wonder where the four or five dull sections of each dinner have gone to, and will raise their heads like well-trained monkeys after the meat course, asking automatically but without much real enthusiasm what kind of pudding there will be *tonight*.

The best answer to that is to have such good food, and such generous casseroles and bowls and platters of it, that there cannot be even a conditioned appetite for more, after the real sensuous human one is satisfied.

Your plan, say, for Mortimer as well as for the others who depend on you for nourishment, includes one meal of starches, one of vegetables or fruits, and one of meat. There are amplifications and refinements to each, naturally [There are indeed many: some human beings bog down with too much meat or too much starch, for instance. Such peculiarities must of course be noted by a loving provider.], but in the main they can be thus simplified.

Breakfast, then, can be toast. It can be piles of toast, generously buttered, and a bowl of honey or jam, and milk for Mortimer and coffee for you. You can be lavish because the meal is so inexpensive. You can have fun, because there is no trotting around with fried eggs and mussy dishes and grease in the pan and a lingeringly unpleasant smell in the air.

Or, on cold mornings, you can have all you want of hot cereal . . . not a pale pabulum made of emasculated wheat, but some brown nutty savorous porridge. Try it with maple syrup and melted butter instead of milk and sugar, once in a while. Or put some raisins or chopped dates in it. It is a sturdy dish, and better than any conventional mélange of tomato juice and toast and this and that and the other, both outside and within you.

If you want Mortimer to drink a fruit juice [I continue to be astonished at the number of people who automatically down a glass of fresh fruit juice, especially before the unavoidable kick of morning coffee. I believe firmly that the combination is pure poison, according to the chemical balance of the one man who, along with several million others, considers it his meat.], you can almost certainly arrange to have it given to him in the middle of the morning or afternoon, when it will not war with the starches in his own middle, and will give him an unadulterated and uncluttered lift.

For lunch, make an enormous salad, in the summer, or a casserole of vegetables, or a heartening and ample soup [. . . with hot tea for the oldsters, and milk at will for everyone . . . and plenty of good buttered toast]. That is all you need, if there is enough of it.

And for dinner, if you want to stick solemnly to your "balanced day," have a cheese soufflé and a light salad, or, if you are in funds, a broiled rare steak and a beautiful platter of sliced herb-besprinkled ripe tomatoes.

That, with some red wine or ale if you like it [and a loaf of honest bread, with or without butter, and toasted or not] and good coffee afterwards, is a meal that may startle your company at first with its simplicity but will satisfy their hunger and their sense of fitness and of balance, all at once. [An unnecessary peptic goad, but a very nice one now and then, is a good soft stinky cheese, a Camembert or Liederkranz, with what is left of the bread, the wine, the hunger.]

And later, when they begin to think of the automatic extravagance of most of our menus, and above all of the ghastly stupid monotony of them, they too will cast off many of their habits, and begin like you to eat the way they *want* to, instead of the way their parents and grandparents taught them. They will be richer, and healthier, and perhaps, best of all, their palates will awaken to new pleasures, or remember old ones. All those things are devoutly to be wished for, now especially.

How to
Catch the Wolf

A creative economy is the fuel of magnificence.
Aristocracy, RALPH WALDO EMERSON

Once during the last war ["The last war" means something different now. I was thirtyish when I wrote this, thinking of 1917 and thereabouts. Now I am infinitely and eons more than forty-ish, and my mind says "next" sooner than "last". . . .] when rationing of sugar and butter had been in effect just long enough to throw all the earnest young housewives into a proper tizzy, my grandmother sat knitting and listening to a small excited group of them discuss with proper pride their various ways of making cake economically. Each felt that her own discovery was the best, of course, and insisted that brown sugar or molasses-with-soda was much better than white, or that if you used enough spices you could substitute bacon fat for butter, or that eggs were quite unnecessary.

Finally my grandmother folded her knitting and then her hands, which was unusual for her because she believed that no real lady's fingers should ever be idle.

"Your conversation is very entertaining, indeed," she said with somewhat more than her ordinary dryness. [People tell me that Grandmother could not possibly have been as unpleasant as I always picture her. Only a psychiatrist would know . . .] "It interests me especially, my dears, because after listening to it this afternoon I see that ever since I was married, well over fifty years ago, I have been living on a war budget without realizing it! I never knew before that using common sense in the kitchen was stylish only in emergencies."

My grandmother's observation need not have been so sardonically phrased (from what I have heard about her she felt it a sign of weakness to be anything but firmly disagreeable most of the time), but probably it was true then . . . and it is even more appropriate now. [As well as *now*, eight years later in so-called Peace Time!]

Every slick magazine in the country is filled with full-page advertisements suggesting that all Americans "try the new thrill of thriftier meat-cuts," and home economics editors in the women's journals are almost incoherent over the exciting discovery that dollars can and should buy more. Vitamins are written and talked about with eager—if at times somewhat confused—enthusiasm, and the old saw that Europe could live on what we throw away rears its inane head in every editorial column. [The word *inane* seems crude and bloodless here, applied to such painful truth. All over the world great piles of wasted potatoes and coffee and tender piglets and dried milk make that truth more shameful, in our economy as well as our hearts.]

In other words, not all women are as sensible as my grandmother . . . until they have to be. Then, I believe, after the first spate of eager bewilderment they can be fully as practical as she, and certainly a lot less grim about it.

It is true that, when the wolf first proves he is actually there, you feel a definite sense of panic. "To work! To work! In heaven's name!"

You talk with your friends. They are either as bewildered as you, or full of what sound like ghastly schemes for living with three other congenial couples and buying all their food from the city dump.

You talk with an older woman, and usually she writes you a long list of recipes full of eggs and cream, both of which give your husband hay fever even if you could afford them, which looks more and more doubtful.

You read magazine articles filled with complicated charts and casual references to thiamin, riboflavin, nonorganic nutritional essentials, and International Units. You try to be serious about them all, and with a dictionary and a pencil you fill in at least the first week on a monthly chart, putting little circles, triangles, and arrows for minerals and vitamins and such, until you see practically the same chart in a rival magazine and realize that it has switched the symbols on you. [I don't think we get as excited about such schemes as we used to. Perhaps that is a bad sign: pills and injections can't do *everything!*]

Out of the murk of misinformation and enthusiasm that bedims even the advertisements in the first months of war (one double-page spread used the words *thrifty* and *thriftier* seventeen times, with an almost breathless sense of discovery!), and the monotony of the articles about what fun it is to buy cheap food and less of it, a better knowledge of each dollar's purchasing power is bound to come.

Women who never thought one way or another about such things before, are going to find that fuel and light, even if they have enough money to pay for them, may be scarce and impossible to hoard, and after the first sense of irritation will learn to cook well and intelligently and economically with very little gas or electricity. [Present-day pottery and kitchenware, available in peacetime, are a wonderful investment for wartime economy. Used intelligently, it makes something as simple as boiling an egg cost half as much as it would in a thin, badly designed utensil, even though a three-minute egg still takes about as long today as it did in 1722.] Magazines give a great many good hints about such thriftiness, usually, and so do other people like my grandmother, and so, in the end, does your own good sense.

It is all a question of weeding out what you yourself like best to do, so that you can live most agreeably in a world full of an increasing number of disagreeable surprises. [Some of them are merely funny, like the carefully sealed cans filled with milk-solids, nitrous-oxide gas, and suchlike, which spit out a "dessert topping" vaguely reminiscent of whipped cream when held correctly downwards, and a fine social catastrophe when sprayed, heedlessly upright, about the room.]

How to Distribute
Your Virtue

Economy is a distributive virtue, and consists not in saving,
but in selection.

Letters to a Noble Lord, EDMUND BURKE, 1796

Almost all people, whether they are potential or actual grandparents, have practiced certain forms of economy in their day,
even if they are not like my own grandmother who practiced it
her whole life. Sometimes their systems have a strange sound
indeed, after the thin days are past and they can look back with
a perspective that is impossible while the wolf seems actually at
the door.

I think especially of one man, moderately famous now as a
deliverer of weighty papers before weightier minds (the kind of
papers, and minds, that are filled with abstruse puns in nine lan-
guages, at least five of which are dead). [The best talker I ever
heard once said to me, "Never ruin a good story by sticking to
the truth." That may be why this one, essentially as it appears
here, has been read in somewhat more embroidered versions,
stitched both by me and by my various loyal friends. The
famous-deliverer-of-weighty-papers himself, wiser if no bet-

ter nourished than so long ago, prefers *this* version.] When he was working on his doctorate in a small French university, he discovered the rather macabre delights of a poverty that could have been depressing to an older tireder man but was gleeful and exciting to him.

He stopped shaving, because he never had any hot water, or sharp razors, or soap, and finally not even a mirror. The result was a fine Old Testament beaver, full of genius.

He bought food at the market on Mondays and Thursdays, after his credit ran out at a succession of lower-than-lowest-grade boardinghouses, and cooked on a one-burner gas plate that was, for some reason, in the outside privy of his mean lodgings.

He began by making himself fairly neat, well-ordered little meals. But washing dishes with no water was a problem, so he found himself using fewer and fewer plates. He was tempted to throw them all away and simply fish things out of the stew-pot with his fingers, but he sensed that man must keep a few barriers between himself and savagery, and compromised on one large soup dish and one spoon.

For several weeks he ate thus in solitary manliness, so pleased with himself and the free good life he was living that he never noticed how ugly and smelly and surly his room and his land-lady were. [Good honest stew is better the second day, and better yet the third. But on the fourth, unless the weather be cool and right. . . .]

Finally, however, inertia and a desire perhaps for complete functionalism overcame him, and he found that rather than ask or hunt for water for his one dish and his one spoon he was eating whatever was in or on them and then spending several minutes licking them clean, very slowly and meticulously, so that they shone and twinkled as much as the cheapest ware can manage to.

He says now, when pressed, that he sat for several minutes on the edge of his bed, and then in a quiet and rather sad way broke the plate so freshly polished, bent the shining spoon into a hoop, went to the corner *coiffeur* and had his beared hacked off, and borrowed enough money to become a boarder again at a moderately bad restaurant. (He also adds with some glee that he was sick as a pup after the first incredibly elaborate meal, after months of monotonous good health and his own spartan stew.) [I know a man who killed another with kindness and too much rich food upon a long-starved stomach. It was clearly accidental manslaughter, not murder, for he had never seen his victim before then, nor heard of him.]

There may be a lesson in this. It sounds rather like it. At least it proves that when he is living with himself a man can do things that in front of other people might seem ugly, or undignified, if he needs to in order to live at all. [I cannot swallow a raw egg in front of anyone in the world, no matter how much I want it. Or so I *think*.]

There are many other ways to save money, some of them written in cookbooks for people to study, and some of them only hidden in the minds of those who might have been hungrier without them. It is good, now when war and its trillion grim surprises haunt all our minds, to talk with other older humans about what they have done in their days to fool the wolf.

One will tell you about hayboxes. Hayboxes are very simple. They are simply strong wooden boxes, one inside another with hay packed between, and if possible a stout covering of linoleum or oilcloth on the outside. You bring whatever food you want to a sturdy boil, put it tightly covered on a layer of hay in the inside box, pack hay all around it, and cover the box securely. [First catch your hay, to paraphrase an old gastronomical adage about hares! Who *has* hay, these days?] Then you count twice as long as your stew or porridge or vegetables would have taken to cook normally, open the haybox, and the food is done. It is primitive, and it is a good thing to know if fuel is a problem for you.

A more modern answer, and a fine one if you can afford the initial expense, is the kind of pressure cooker that looks like a Dutch oven with a whistle on top. It does almost miraculous things: string beans are cooked in three minutes, a Swiss steak is tender and juicy and full of flavor in but a few more, and on and on. It reduces cooking time to an almost boring minimum . . . which of course is worth it if you are skimping on gas or working in a munitions factory with neither time nor inclination for the pleasures of the kitchen.

Another amateur economist will tell you of countless ways to make little seem like more. Most of them sound foul, after a few minutes of such reminiscences, but in practice they are trustworthy, if not admirable esthetically. For instance, you can make scrambled eggs "go a lot further" by putting bread crumbs in them when they are a little more than half done, and as a matter of fact if you use decent crumbs [say, of homemade bread or of an honorable pumpernickel] the eggs have a very good flavor indeed, and a nice texture. Or in a soufflé, add one cup of puffed cereal to the three separated eggs, and you will have food for four people [. . . at least three of whom, I feel impelled to add, you dislike intensely and hope never to see again].

Another trick is to cut the consumption of sugar in half when you are making jams and preserves by mixing one cup of sugar with every two cups of fruit and the correct amount of water, and then adding one-half a teaspoonful of bicarbonate of soda. I have never done this, but ardent housewives who lived through the last war in both England and America swear that it works, and of course the wear and tear on sugar cards is cut down considerably. [Another way, of course, is by now almost universal: pectin. I hate it. I swear I can always detect it, by the ugly solid dull grainy look of anything that contains it. I would rather eat one spoonful of jelly made with fruit and sugar than a dozen of the other stuff. Or perhaps vice versa.]

As for butter and other shortenings, I have always felt that I should prefer too little of the best to plenty of an inferior kind. However, there are many families who are used to a great deal of pastries and fried foods, and who find it difficult to forgo them. There are several reputable substitutes, not only for butter, but for butter substitutes! [It is said that scientists are evolving a new and excellent salad- and cooking-oil made from grapefruit skins.]

If you use oil or lard for deep frying, never let it smoke much, but use when it is bluish and not moving on the surface. If you eat much bacon, save the fat, and pour it always into a metal container and then pour water over it. The burned food particles will sink into the water, and the fat will rise as it cools and be clean and easy to lift into another cup or bowl. Such fat should be kept in a cool and dark place, as should olive oil if you are lucky enough to own any, but never in an icebox.

As for your icebox. (It is easiest to take it for granted that you still have one, and that it works, and that it is not an annex for the local Red Cross and filled to bulging with blood plasma.) [This is one of the doggedly cold reminders that this current war is, or so everyone tells me, *cold*. . . .] As for your icebox, then, there are several ways to use it with the most intelligence.

Of course, keeping it clean eliminates waste from spoiled food, and defrosting it regularly makes it use surprisingly less fuel, if it is an automatic one. Never put meat or other foods in it in their store-wrappings; they use extra cold and are less good. Almost the same is true of butter, which should be taken from its box but left in its thin paper protection or else put into a covered dish. Vegetables should always be washed if they are to be stored in the box, and lettuce and other salads should have the white cores cut out. Little green onions and such sturdy herbs as parsley can be kept fresh and pungent for a long time if they are washed and drained and put into tightly covered jars, and it is a nice feeling to know that they are there, ready for use, whenever you want them (which will be oftener than you realize, once you have caught the habit).

If you cook rice or such pastes as spaghetti and macaroni very often, you can keep them from boiling over and at the same time lay the foundation for a decent soup by putting in about a teaspoonful of butter or suet or oil. [Quote now that the war is over hah hah unquote, I would add about three times that much fat to the pot.] After you have drained what you are cooking, save the water and cook it again with a little onion, some meat stock if you have it, or a couple of bouillon cubes, and you have a nutritious broth that would shame nobody.

When you cook such things as rice, or potatoes or spaghetti or any of the starches, cook enough for two meals instead of one. It costs about the same, in heat consumption, and you have the food ready to heat in various ways and serve again, a few days later. [Ah, rice pudding, rich with raisins! Ah, spaghetti baked with honey and shaved almonds in a buttery dish! Ah, potatoes any way at all but perhaps especially mixed with egg and cheese and fried! Ah.] (The same is true of almost everything; most vegetables, for instance, are delicious chilled in salads, especially if you have put them aside without buttering them.)

More or less, this simple but surprisingly little-practiced rule is true in using an oven: try to fill every inch of space in it. Even if you do not want baked apples for supper, put a pan of them with whatever is baking at from 250 to 400 degrees. They will be all the better for going slowly, but as long as their skins do not scorch they can cook fast. They make a good meal in themselves, with cream if you have any, or milk heated with some cinnamon and nutmeg in it, and buttered toast and tea.

Another thing to do while the oven is going is to put in a pan of thinly sliced that is too stale to use anymore. It makes good Melba toast, if you watch it so that it does not get too brown. If you want to you can soak it first in water or watery milk with a little sugar in it, or even a little salt and pepper, to make zwieback that is very good indeed with soup or tea. [These petty tricks seem somewhat more so when gas flows through the pipes and firewood is available and electricity actually turns on with a button. But in each one of them there is a basic thoughtfulness, a searching for the kernel in the nut, the bite in honest bread, the slow savor in a baked wished-for apple. It is this thoughtfulness that we must hold to, in peace or war, if we may continue to eat to live.]

Or you can roast some walnuts in their shells, and eat them while they are still pretty hot, with fresh cold apples and a glass of port if possible, for one of the desserts most conducive in this world to good conversation.

While these various shortcuts to economy are simmering and fuming in their borrowed heat, you can be roasting a large joint of beef, which will seem expensive beyond reason when you pay for it but which will last a long time if your family is of normal size and appetite. Potatoes can be baked around its pan, about an hour before it is done, and if their skins are oiled and they are pricked when they are taken from the oven they will not grow soggy and may even be used after they are cold, if they are good potatoes, for a casserole or a salad.

Or you can cook what the home economists love to call a "one-dish meal," a "coordinated dinner," or, less genteelly, a casserole. This, if it is intelligently planned and seasoned, can be delicious (and will leave fine fundaments for another meal tomorrow, unless it is already at work using up yesterday's.)

For instance, make a Baked Ham Slice. [This, I notice eight years later, is clearly documented on page 97. My main comment on it is monotonous: I like it. My main change would be to use cider or white wine for the cup of water. And any kitchen-idiot would know enough to core the apples.] Get a little more meat than you plan to use at dinner, because it is fine the next day diced in a macaroni-and-cheese casserole, or in an omelet or any way you want it.

A green salad is good with this, and either a light beer or a rather sharp white wine. And for dessert, if you want one, nothing can be a better complement to the tang of ham and apples than hot gingerbread, the dark kind that springs practically full-born from a paper carton and the gracious shadow of Mary Ball Washington [it says on the advertisement], or can be made a little better and a little less expensively from a trusted recipe of my mother's, called Edith's Gingerbread. The recipe is given on page 158. [A quick but thoughtful look forward confirms my belief that this is the best recipe for gingerbread ever devised. Farewell, gracious packaged shadow of Mary Ball Washington!]

A little sherry poured over the bread while it is hot makes it even better, if you plan to eat it all at once, with sweet butter too if possible. If not, a simple wine sauce or a hard sauce is good.

If there is any gingerbread left, it is almost better cold than hot. When it gets stale (although I have never known any to last that long), it is delicious split open and toasted, for tea. [Tea? Who drinks tea anymore? It used to be something "people" did: the gentle ritual, the delicate ceremony. For me it meant a discreet adolescent gobbling of cakes and cookies, nigh unto my thirtieth year, while older wiser creatures sipped alongside. Now? Now I could not face a saffron-bun or a plum-heavy . . . and tea makes me drunk.]

And what ham is left, if you don't like macaroni and cheese, you can dice and put in a buttered casserole the next day with cooked noodles, and a small can of mushrooms, browned in shortening. Season it with salt and fresh-ground pepper, and heat thoroughly (small ramekins take less heat than a big casserole). This makes another "one-dish meal," with a salad, cheese, and coffee.

While the oven is cooking the ham, you can be baking some clean sweet potatoes or yams in their skins, and either a pan of apples or another cake, or anything else that takes a moderately slow oven. Then, in a couple of days, you can make some such hearty dessert as Sweet Potato Pudding.

Or mash and season the peeled yams, put in a buttered shallow pan, and cover with little sausages which have been brought to the boil in plain water. Put in a hot oven until the sausages are thoroughly cooked and brown, at least twenty minutes.

A surprisingly good cake, which I loved so much in the last war that I dreamed about it at night, and which I have tried on this war's children with practically the same results, can be whipped together and put in the oven with the ham and whatever else you are storing up for the week ahead. It is called War Cake, for want of a pleasanter name, and is a rather crude moist dark loaf that keeps well and costs little. [I seem to have said at least twice in this book that I dreamed about War Cake at night. On rereading page 154 I am inclined to suggest a touch of indigestion and change "dream" to "nightmare." The trouble is that I know the recipe to be excellent.]

Sliced thin with a glass of milk, it is a pleasant lunch. Or it can be sliced and toasted, basted with sherry, and served hot with wine sauce for a good dessert, once it seems somewhat past its prime. [Wonderful example of understatement! I really mean: "When the cake is curled, stiff, and apparently unusable."]

The absorbing and profitable pastime of seeing how many things you can cook at once in an oven is almost as good applied to the top of the stove, especially if you have a steam-cooker or even a roomy Dutch oven. Then you can cook several vegetables at once, or less economically but still with a certain amount of good sense cook each one separately, one after another, using the same pot and the same steam, so that at the end you have several things ready for reheating through the week, and a fine heady broth that will do wonders with any dish that calls for stock or even plain water.

It is best to keep it in an old gin bottle in the icebox, alongside the other old gin bottle filled with juices left from canned fruit. You can add what's left of the morning tomato juice. You can squeeze in the last few drops of the lemon you drink in hot water before breakfast, if you still do that. You can put canned vegetable juices in. You can steep parsley stems in hot water and pour their juice into the bottle. In other words, never throw away any vegetable or its leaves or its juices unless they are bad; else count yourself a fool. [That's right!]

If you keep your old gin bottle cold and reasonably on the move it need never spoil nor be anything but a present help in time of trouble, and a veritable treasure jug for vitamins and minerals that otherwise would have gone down the drain. [That's *so* right!]

Sometimes try a glassful, no matter from what vegetables, fresh-cooked or canned, you may have salvaged it, diluted if you wish with tomato juice or a little lemon and seasoning. It will make you feel astonishingly energetic—almost human, really [. . . a condition devoutly to be aimed for, given our basic state].

All vegetables, whether they are steam-cooked or not, should be done as quickly as possible, and in as little water. In this way at least fifty percent of the minerals are collected in the water. They should be drained at once, and either prepared for serving or allowed to cool for the icebox and another day. If they are to be used later, they should be underdone rather than tender, since the reheating will cook them again; and of course they should not be seasoned and buttered until they are ready to be used, except for the herbs you may have cooked with them. [I know a little more now and would seldom cook herbs with vegetables I planned to use another day. I would add them *that* day.]

Vegetables cooked for salads should always be on the crisp side, like those trays of zucchini and slender green beans and cauliflowerets in every *trattoria* in Venice, in the days when the Italians could eat correctly. You used to choose the things you wanted: there were tiny potatoes in their skins, remember, and artichokes boiled in olive oil, as big as your thumb, and much tenderer . . . and then the waiter would throw them all into an ugly white bowl and splash a little oil and vinegar over them, and you would have a salad as fresh and tonic to your several senses as La Primavera. It can still be done, although never in the same typhoidic and enraptured air. You can still find little fresh vegetables, and still know how to cook them until they are not quite done, and chill them, and eat them in a bowl. [Why do we not do this oftener, much time as it will take? I am tired of "tossed green salads," no matter what their subtleties of flavor. I want a salad of a dozen tiny vegetables: rosy potatoes in their tender skins, asparagus tips, pod-peas, beans two inches long and slender as thick hairs. . . . I want them cooked, each alone, to fresh perfection. I want them dressed, all together, in a discreet veil of oil and condiments. Why not? What, in peacetime, is to prevent it? Are we too busy being peaceful for such play?]

You can still live with grace and wisdom, thanks partly to the many people who write about how to do it and perhaps talk overmuch about riboflavin and economy, and partly to your own innate sense of what you must do with the resources you have, to keep the wolf from snuffing too hungrily through the keyhole.

How to Boil Water

"Here, Miss," I says, "what d'ye call this?" "Soup, Sir,"
she says. "Soup? Soup? Well, blast me then!" I says,
polite-like. "Is this what I've been sailin' on for the
past fifty years?"

The Peppery Sayings of an Old Salt,
HENRY TREWELYAN, 1869

I

There was a semiapocryphal figure, in my childhood, who
could not even boil water. I forget who she was: a Southern girl,
I think, who went to finishing school in Virginia with my
mother.

"Oh," my mother used to say, snorting a little and tossing her
head half scornfully and half with a kind of wistful envy, "*oh,*
she couldn't even boil water!" Then my mother would add,
". . . before she was married!"

For a long time I believed that the first pangs of connubial
bliss brought with them a new wisdom, a kind of mystic
knowledge that slipped with the wedding ring over all the fingers of the bride, so that at last and suddenly and completely she
knew how to boil water.

Now, I believe otherwise. Now, I believe that few women, Southern or not, even virgins or not, ever realize the spacious limits of putting water in a pot and boiling it. When is water boiling? When, indeed, is water water?

Water is water, Webster says, when it is a colorless, inodorous, transparent fluid, consisting of two volumes of hydrogen to one of oxygen. It can also be rain, or the sea, or a diamond's luster. The water I mean, though . . . the water the Southern maiden couldn't boil . . . is the clear good water that flows from a tap, or if you are lucky from a spring or well. It is the best for cooking wolves.

And when is water boiling? It can be said, with few people to argue the point, that water boils when it has been heated to two hundred and twelve degrees Fahrenheit. Myself, I would say that when it bubbles with large energetic bubbles, and looks ready to hop from the kettle, and makes a rocky rather than a murmuring noise, and sends off a deal of steam, it is boiling. [A friend of mine who grew up alongside a samovar has only one way to describe water proper for tea: "A *mad* boil." In the same forceful way she never says rolls or toast must be hot, or very hot. They must be "hot-hot-*hot!*" This is pronounced as much as possible like a one-syllable sound of intense excitement, about no matter how dull a bun.]

At this point, full of sound and fury, it is ready to be used, given, of course, that it has been prepared in a clean vessel for some purpose other than the purely scientific one of discovering when it would boil. Most people, whether or not they are married and therefore prescient, as I so long ago thought they would be about water at least, do not know that there is one moment at which it is *au point*, and then all the rest of the time it is overdone, most as surely as is a broiled steak or a *crêpe suzette*.

The quaint old fiction of the kettle simmering all day on the hearth, waiting to be turned into a delicious cup of tea, is actively disturbing to anyone who cares very much whether his tea will be made from lively water instead of a liquid that in spite of its apparent resemblance to Webster's definition is flat, exhausted, tasteless—in other words, with the hell cooked out of it. [Altitude changes the sound, as well as the speed, of boiling water. There seems to be more noise, high up.]

It is safe to say that when the water boils, as it surely will, given enough heat under it, it is ready. Then, at that moment and no other, pour it into the teapot or over or around or into whatever it is meant for, whatever calls for it. If it cannot be used then, turn off the heat and start over again when you yourself are ready; it will harm you less to wait than it will the water to boil too long.

And now, irrespective of your virginity or lack of it, you may consider yourself able to boil water. Nobody will ever shake her head about you, as my mother still does occasionally about the Southern girl; or if heads are shaken now and then, at least you will know that it is not because your tea is made with an overdone mélange of hydrogen and oxygen.

II

The natural progression from boiling water to boiling water with something in it can hardly be avoided, and in most cases is heartily to be wished for. As a steady diet, plain water is inclined to make thin fare, and even saints, of which there are an unexpected number these days, will gladly agree that a few herbs and perhaps a carrot or two and maybe a bit of meager bone on feast-days can mightily improve the somewhat monotonous flavor of the hot liquid.

Soup, in other words, is good. [As a matter of fact, soup is even better, in my gastronomy, than it was nine years ago. This is due partly to my increased knowledge of its ever-changing structure, and partly to my own increased age. A good hot broth is more welcome now, and will be more so in yet another decade . . . or two or three!]

It is probably the oldest cooked food on the earth, after roasted meat (in spite of the great Maître Escoffier's dictum that "the nutritious liquids known under the name of Soups are of comparatively recent origin and as now served do not date any farther back than the early years of the nineteenth century").

How it was discovered is best left unpondered except by radio scriptwriters and people who try to interest children in the Stone Age. Its inevitable progress from a pot with a watery bone in it to potage à la Reine and Crème Vichysoisse is for anyone to read in forty thousand cookbooks, most of them bad. [By now there must be fifty thousand, most of them still bad, or at least dull. It is safe to wager that in the past eight years not more than eight really important cookbooks have been published in America . . . and that, of those, not more than one is *essential*. (At first I wrote: "Not *one*.")]

"Certain fundamental rules must be carefully assimilated before one can learn all the requirements for making a truly excellent soup stock," one gastronomist writes, and then goes on to give a good if elaborate ritual. Probably the best of these is Sheila Hibben's, in her *Kitchen Manual*; the result is as clear, rich, and comforting as her own prose, and worthy to be well studied by anyone who wants at least a nodding acquaintance with *la haute cuisine*. It is probably unfortunate that such classical procedures as hers and Mrs. Moody's and Escoffier's for making the basic stock will become increasingly good escape-reading material in direct ratio to the possibility of following them in our small kitchens and hurried hours.

Another drawback to this, and probably the most important one for people who are pondering how best to cook the wolf that sniffs through the keyhole every night about twelve-thirty [My own wolf, by now almost a member of the family, presently sniffs loudest about four in the morning. The change in his hours is variously ascribed to modern-day tension, daylight saving, and glandular change (mine, not his). He still sounds hungry.] is that by the time you have taken a day off and assembled the necessary ingredients and used enough fuel to braise them, simmer them, boil them, and clarify them properly, you have spent a fair portion of the week's food budget. The result is good, but Man should not live on consommé alone, and if you make the stock as you are told to, there will be very little money left for anything else.

A great deal of misinformation has been quoted for several centuries about the delicious soup that sits for years at the back of every good French stove. It is supposed to be like old-fashioned yeast, always renewing itself and yet always stemming from the original "starter," so that a chicken bone thrown in last Easter may long since have disappeared but will still lend its aromatic aura to the present brew.

I do not like this fiction, and prefer not to believe it. I think soup-pots should be made fresh now and then, like people's minds at the New Year. They should be emptied and scrubbed and started over again, with clean water, a few peppercorns, whatever little scraps are left from yesterday, and then today's bones and lettuce leaves and cold toast and such. Set at the back of the stove and left to simmer, with an occasional stir from the cook, they can make a fine clear stock for sauces as well as a heartening broth.

And . . .

In the country, or wherever there is a big kitchen with constant heat in the stove, they are economical. Otherwise they are foolish and outmoded, and will make fuel bills rise and apartments smell.

People who work whether in offices or Red Cross rooms, must glean what nostalgic comfort they can from merely reading Escoffier and Hibben and the others, and resign themselves (without too much difficulty, I hope!) to some such potage as the following, which costs little, takes even less time to make, and has infinite variations, according to the state of the vegetable bin.

Chinese Consommé

2 cups beef or chicken consommé (1 can) or vegetable juice saved from cooking	1 green onion and stalk, sliced very thin and/or a few very thin slices of whatever vegetable lurks in the bin, such as squash, cucumber, radish, etc.
2 cups (1 can) tomato juice	
1 stalk celery sliced very thin	
½ cup dry white wine (or juice of ½ lemon)	1 tablespoon butter or olive oil

Heat the consommé and tomato juice. Put everything else in a hot tureen or casserole, pour the soup over, and serve at once. The nearly transparent rounds and crescents of the raw vegetables float on the top, and with the wine give a delicate flavor that seldom needs other seasoning.

This consommé, in spite of the fact that it need not even have meat broth in it, is very stimulating, as well as beautiful to look at, and could never be dismissed as thin, the way Abraham Lincoln did a "homeopathic soup that was made by boiling the shadow of a pigeon that had been starved to death." It is an appetizing first course; with buttered toast and perhaps baked apples and cream to follow it makes a simple pleasant supper.

Another good consommé which takes little time is a variant of the onion soup of blessed memory you used to drink early in the morning at Les Halles, after you'd watched the last of the big wagons piled with baby carrots and round satiny onions unload and trundle off again. (Was it you, or was it someone else you remember meeting once in a dream . . . a long peaceful dream, but beautiful and exciting too.)

[I have found only one onion soup I could not like, a rich, cloying, thickened puree, brown but not brown enough, served for the diehards like me at second-rate balls in French Switzerland. They were indeed routs, given for the benefit of everything from laryngitic yodelers to needy edelweiss-hounds, always in beautiful dusty old abandoned casinos, always with good champagne and "jazz-hot" bands down from Paris. I was an habituée. But I couldn't stand the predawn soup. . . .

All other soup recipes called *onion* are, so far, all right. Ambrose Heath has some reliable beauties in his little classic named, bluntly, *Good Soups*. His best is probably No. 1, which he ends with the wonderful cook-to-cook statement: "It is the soup of soups." He also gives Mrs. Glasse's recipe (1767), and quotes my favorite, which I have never been able, for fair reasons or foul, to essay. He refers to it somewhat ambiguously as *peculiar*. I can state more openly that it has haunted me since I first read it in Paul Reboux's *Nouvelle Cuisine* many years ago; that it contains, beside the requisite onions, dry champagne, half a ripe Camembert, several beaten eggs, and thirty well-skinned walnuts; that in my edition of the fantastic collection of recipes it ends, "Eat between 3 and 4 A.M. for optimism."

On second thought, and after due consideration of M. Reboux's suggestions, I think the safe sane eminently *basic* recipe that follows should stand alone. May the printers forgive me . . . !]

Parisian Onion Soup

2 *cans (1 quart) beef broth or consommé*	1 *heaping tablespoon flour*
	rye bread, sliced thin and toasted
2 *or 3 sweet onions, sliced very thin*	*grated snappy cheese (Parmesan type)*
3 *tablespoons butter or good oil*	

*Brown the onions in the fat, sprinkle with flour, and stir while it sim-
mers for 10 minutes. Add the soup, preferably heated, and let boil
slowly until the onion is very tender. Spread the cheese thickly on the
toast, and melt under a quick broiler. (This is better than putting the
toast and cheese on the soup and then melting, since the toast stays crisp-
er.) Pour the soup into a hot tureen, cover with the toast, and serve at
once.*

This is what might be called a "light but hearty" soup, and with
a good salad and fruit and coffee would please any hungry family. [All cookbooks are interesting, at least to me, but I think
some of the most readable of them have been written about
soups (Ambrose Heath's, Mrs. Mabon's), just as often the best
section of a comprehensive book like Escoffier's may concern
the same infinitely variable subject.]

There are many others, which are even more a complete meal
in themselves, and which like all such dishes can be changed according to the will and pocketbook of the chef. Here is a basic
recipe for chowders, which can be stretched this way or that and
made country-simple or town-elegant.

Chowder

½ pound lean bacon or salt pork, cut in small cubes	½ cup rich cream (optional)
2 large onions, chopped fine	1 small can chopped pimientos (optional)
½ green pepper chopped fine (optional)	1 can whole-kernel corn or 1 can chopped clams or 1 can tomato-pulp or whatever else you can think of
3 cups water	
3 large potatoes, cut in small cubes	
salt and pepper as desired	

*Fry the bacon until crisp. Add the onions and green pepper and brown
well. Add the water, and bring to a boil. Put in the potatoes and let cook*

slowly until tender. Add the rest of the ingredients, heat thoroughly, and serve. [If this is too thick, fish stock or more water or more cream can be added. My father likes to stand a spoon in this, but I myself prefer it somewhat wetter.]

There are some proud boosters of regional cookery who say that a chowder made with anything but crumbled soda crackers is heinous and insulting. They can but ignore the potatoes, then, and substitute their chosen thickener, and feel happy.

There is another well-worn controversy among chowder-lovers as to which is correct, the kind made with milk or the kind made with tomato and water. Long ago it may have been dependent on transportation and climate and so forth, so that in the winter when the cow was still fresh there was milk, and in the summer when the tomatoes were plump and heavy they were used. . . .

Who knows? Furthermore, who cares? You should eat according to your own tastes, as much as possible, and, if you want to make a chowder with milk *and* tomato, and crackers *and* potatoes, do it, if the result pleases you (which sounds somewhat doubtful, but possible).

Once the Vicomte de Mauduit remarked to somebody, or perhaps somebody remarked to the Vicomte de Mauduit, that eating is an art worthy to rank with the other methods by which man chooses to escape from reality. Stripped of its slightly pontifical rhythm, this statement sounds quite true. And one of its strange proofs, in some ways, is the present vogue for vichyssoise.

This bland unctuous broth, served in a hundred modish restaurants from New York to San Francisco, seems in some mysterious way to soothe the throbbing minds of today's children even as it calmed the outraged stomachs of yesterday's aristocratic grandfathers, who absorbed it willy-nilly by prescription at Vichy and Baden-Baden, instead of ordering it eagerly at the Ruban Bleu or Jack's.

There seems to be something about its robust delicacy, its frigid smoothness, its slightly vulgar but so dainty sprinkling of chives on the white surface, that makes even young-ancient metropolites with sinus trouble or other occupational diseases forget the age they live in, and sit back refreshed and quiet for a minute or two.

It is too bad that this current piece of gastronomical voodoo is so expensive and complicated to make—at least, like Mrs. Hibben's classical consommé, *correctly*. The cream must have exactly twenty-four percent fat content: sometimes the mixture should be at 196° Fahrenheit, sometimes at 212° Fahrenheit. One-sixteenth of a teaspoonful of ground mace must be added at just the correct moment.

However, there are compromises that can be admitted, whether you approve of them or not. Here is a recipe, a combination really of Escoffier's Soupe à la Bonne Femme and one I found in a calendar published by the gas company in the Canton of Vaud in Switzerland. It is excellent hot, but to make it into a mighty passable vichysoisse it should have some cream [sour, or very thick] beaten into it and be put into the coldest part of the icebox for at least twenty-four hours.

Cream of Potato Soup

4 medium potatoes, peeled and sliced thin	salt and pepper
2 mild onions, sliced thin	1 cup potato water
2 tablespoons flour	3 cups rich scalded milk
4 tablespoons butter (no compromise here)	1 tablespoon chopped parsley
	1 tablespoon chopped chives if possible

Stew the onions gently in one-half the butter for 15 minutes. Add the potatoes and cover with a small amount of water, about 2 cups. Cook gently until tender. Drain, saving 1 cup of the water, and put the veg-etables through a strainer. [A fine strainer. I notice increasingly that most average cooks, of which or whom I am one, grow careless about sieves and strainers. They usually compromise, after a few years in the kitchen, with one general-utility implement that will cope more or less with their normal duties. Tut, tut, tut! (Shall go to the hardware store tomorrow . . . no, today!)]

Make a roux of the remaining butter and the flour, add the potato water and the seasoning, and stir in the scalded milk. Combine this mix-ture with the strained vegetables and heat thoroughly, beating with an eggbeater for several minutes. Add the chopped herbs and serve at once. (Or chill and serve next day as vichysoisse.)

There is another kind of soup, certainly not bland but with a freakish appeal to it [I do not know why I said freakish. This soup, which is more widely served each summer in America, is as respectable as any Yankee chowder.] that should be served as icy-cold as vichysoisse and might well act as an alternative to those weary brittle souls who live through the summer months in any city, thanks mainly to what their grandmothers probably called "cold potato cream." It is simple to make, and inexpen-sive, and unlike vichysoisse is fairly elastic, depending in the main on how fortunate you are in growing or buying herbs.

This recipe stems partly from Paul Reboux and partly from a Spanish chef on an Italian freighter that once ran between Mar-seille and Portland, Oregon.

Gazpacho

[Within the past few years I have found myself involved in a discussion, esoteric as well as practical, about the correct way to make a gazpacho. I still stay loyal to this recipe, while accentuating the fact that it, like rules for all good native soups, can vary with each man who makes it.]

1 *generous mixed handful of chives, chervil, parsley, basil, marjoram . . . any or all, but* fresh	1 *small glass olive oil (or really flavorful nut oil or substitute) juice of 1 lemon*
1 *garlic clove*	1 *mild onion, sliced paper-thin*
1 *sweet pepper, pimiento or bell*	1 *cup diced cucumber salt and pepper*
2 *peeled and seeded tomatoes*	½ *cup bread crumbs*

Chop the herbs and mash thoroughly with the garlic, pimiento, and to-matoes, adding the oil very slowly, and the lemon juice. Add about 3 glasses of cold water [I still say this is the correct liquid. But often I use good meat or fish stock.] or as much as you wish. Put in the onion and the cucumber, season, sprinkle with bread crumbs, and ice for at least 4 hours before serving.

This gazpacho can be altered to fit what comes from the garden, but it should always have oil and garlic and lemon juice and herbs rubbed heavily together [this is the important trick: a kind of thick marinade, really, of the macerated herbs, oil, acid . . .] and onion and some other vegetable floating around in it; and it should be very cold indeed. Then it is a perfect summer soup, tantalizing, fresh, and faintly perverse as are all primitive dishes eaten by too-worldly people.

It is good for lunch, or for supper. [In hot Spain ice cubes float in it. Most Americans shy away from this strangeness, I find.] It is especially good if you have a barbecue, and want some le-gitimate and not too alcoholic way to keep your guests busy while you turn the steak: put a big tureen of it on the table, and let them serve themselves into cups, and eat toasted crusts with it if they want to. Then when you declare the entrée done, whether it be filet or ground-round patties, you will find ap-petites sharp and wits fairly clear, and a satisfying patina of conversation glimmering in the air. [I always see to it that I have made too much gazpacho. It ripens well, when kept chilled, and is a soul-satisfying thing to drink, chilled, midway in a torrid morning. It is also one of the world's best breakfasts for unfortunates who are badly hung over.]

[Another fine summer soup is made by the following recipe. It is one of my growing number of Things I Do Not Mention Gastronomically. If I tell the smiling people who sip at it that it is made of mashed shrimps and especially *buttermilk*, they wince, gag, hurry away. So I say nothing, and serve it from invisible hogsheads to unconscious but happy hordes.

Cold Buttermilk Soup

1 ½ *pounds shrimps, cooked and* *chopped*	1 *tablespoon prepared mustard*
½ *medium cucumber, finely* *diced*	1 *teaspoon salt*
1 *tablespoon minced fresh dill*	1 *teaspoon sugar*
	1 *quart buttermilk*

Mix together shrimps, cucumber and seasonings; stir in buttermilk and chill thoroughly. Yield: 6 portions.]

III

Probably the most satisfying soup in the world for people who are hungry, as well as for those who are tired or worried or cross or in debt or in a moderate amount of pain or in love or in robust health or in any kind of business huggermuggery, is minestrone.

Minestrone, according to some devotees, must of necessity be based on a bean broth. Others say that minestrone started with a puree of dried soaked cooked beans is not minestrone at all, but minestra. Still others say that: 1. It must be seasoned with vegetables that have been glazed with a generous handful of diced ham or bacon. 2. It must never be breathed upon by meat in any form. The same question exists about adding or not adding small cooked pasta like broken spaghetti at the last minute. There are probably other differences, for like all basically pure and honest dishes it has as many interpretations as it has makes.

Always, though, it is a thick unsophisticated soup, heartwarming and soul-staying, full of aromatic vegetables and well bound at the last with good cheese. "A plate of this pottage," Mrs. Mazza once wrote, "topped with grated Romano, served with crisp garlicked sour-dough bread, a salad and a glass of wine, and *I have dined.*"

This soup is an economical one, partly because it is even better the second or third day than it was the first, and what may have seemed a rather long cooking time really averages but a few minutes for each serving. Onions, garlic, potatoes, and young cabbage are almost always in the markets or your own vegetable bins, and any other vegetables in season may be added with impunity. Fresh ones are best, undoubtedly, but frozen ones can be kept, a little from each package, for the weekly or bimonthly minestrone, and even canned ones are better than none, if you really want to arm your moral and physical guts with this somewhat finicky but all-satisfying soup.

A Basic Minestrone

½	pound bacon or salt pork or fat ham	2	cups tomatoes, peeled	
1	small onion, chopped	1	teaspoon fresh basilico	op-tional
1	stalk chopped celery	1	teaspoon oregano	but
1	handful chopped parsley	1	teaspoon sweet basil	nice

Soften onion in heated meat-fat, add celery, parsley, and herbs, and stir for 10 minutes, to make a glaze, adding a little water if necessary to keep from sticking.

Add the tomato, stirring constantly and taking care not to burn.

Stir in 2 or 3 quarts of water. Add a little mace if you like it. (This soup is fun, because it's so malleable!)

Put at least the first 5 of the following vegetables through the fine grinder of the vegetable chopper [Or cut them not too finely, let them simmer until tender, and then mash them well with a potato masher before you add any pasta. I like this method better than the one I gave before.] and add them to the soup:

2 *large onions*	6 *stalks celery*
1 *potato, skin and all*	*some spinach . . . say, a big*
1 *(or 2) cloves garlic*	*handful*
½ *small cabbage (Savoy*	*some green beans . . . the*
preferably)	*same*
3 *carrots*	*(You see what I mean?)*

Bring the whole thing slowly to a boil, and then let simmer until the vegetables are very tender. Add some pasta 20 minutes before serving if you like it (not until the next day if you plan to use the minestrone more than once). Churn the soup ferociously, and serve over thin toasted bread or not, but always with a good ample bowl of grated dry cheese to sprinkle upon each serving, as the pleased human who eats it may desire.

For the rest of the meal, Mrs. Mazza and I are as one. There is no point doing much else, the night you make minestrone, because nobody will eat anything else anyway. Save your tarts for a leaner hungrier night.

IV

There are many variations of any recipe for a soup that includes chopped vegetables. They depend on the ingenuity of the cook and the size of the purse . . . not to mention a few other things like climate and war, and even political leanings. (I know several earnest thoughtful women who would rather see their children peaked than brew something with the foreign name mine-strone, because in this year of 1942 the United States is at war with Italy. There is a fundamental if tiring truth about all this, and you and I can only hope that right will conquer over might before too long.) [In the 1950s some people feel helplessly antagonistic to *borscht*! Fortunately, I do not.]

If by any chance you cannot or do not like or do not want to like minestrone as such, I suggest that you try this wholesome variant, which itself can be changed somewhat to suit your garden but obviously is best when its ingredients are cheapest at home or in the market:

Green Garden Soup

2	tablespoons butter or good oil	1	handful parsley
1	bunch watercress	2	cans (4 cups) chicken or beef
½	head lettuce		broth
3	small onions and tops	1	egg yolk
2	or 3 cabbage leaves	½	cup thick cream (also if
4	celery-stalk tops		possible)
1	sprig thyme or marjoram if		seasoning
	possible		

Chop or grind [I think every kitchen should have a good mortar-and-pestle. My own is wooden, but I would like a stone one someday.] the vegetables (clean, of course). Heat them gently for about 10 minutes with the oil, and add broth. Cover and simmer slowly until very tender, about 45 minutes. Beat egg yolk and cream together, and add after the soup is in the tureen. Sprinkle with freshly ground black pepper.

[A much more elegant version of this trustworthy Green Garden Soup is the following one, which depends not only on certain unchanging ingredients (mainly sorrel) but on the almost Chinese urgency of its timing.

It was first made for me by a handsome woman in San Francisco who had once been prima ballerina in second-rate cities all around the Mediterranean . . . a wearing life that apparently made child's play of her cooking and serving eight-course finicky dinners.

I have concocted her soup often since I met her, but never with her unflustered gracefulness. For her I call this Potage Else, rather than her more unconsciously (and modestly) pontifical Potage Bonne Femme "Esquin."

Potage Else

3 *tablespoons butter*	2 *tablespoons flour*
3 *sprigs parsley*	2 *quarts rich veal stock, boiling*
3 *leaves lettuce*	4 *egg yolks*
1 *medium onion*	1 *cup cream*
1 *pint sorrel*	*chervil, if possible*
nutmeg, salt, pepper	

Melt butter in large saucepan. Finely chop parsley, lettuce, onion, sorrel, and add with pinch of nutmeg and salt and pepper to pan. Cover closely and let wilt over slow heat for 10 minutes. Add flour and mix well. Gradually add 2 quarts of boiling stock. Add a little minced chervil, if available. Let the whole boil 10 minutes. Beat the eggs, mix thoroughly with the cream, and add this liaison *slowly to the soup, stirring constantly.* Do not allow to boil again. *Serve at once.]*

[One delicious soup I have gradually evolved is made of about one quart of garden lettuces, scallions, parsley, herbs, all chopped fine and then ground to paste in the mortar. Slowly I add seasoning and one quart of rich milk, and then chill it very well . . . for a summer lunch.]

On the other hand, if you say phooie to the whole school of minestrone and feel that chopped vegetables have their rightful place only on the trays of toothless infants and gaffers, your best procedure is one of experimentation.

First install a solid and well-known can-opener in a sensible place in your kitchen: above or to one side of the sink, for instance. (Of course I mention the kind that works like an old-fashioned sidewinder victrola, since any other, to my mind, is a potential source of bad temper, a dirty floor, and finally blood poisoning.) [Most of them now, to the mutual benefit of the manufacturer and the cook, fasten to the wall with a gadget that enables you to put up an ice crusher (fine in summer), a knife sharpener (wonderful any time at all), and so on. They are a good investment.]

After your fairly expensive opener has been firmly screwed into place, prepare to collect dividends from it as long as your arm can crank it and you can find things in cans to buy. Fill one shelf, if you can afford it, with tinned soups to start with: nationally advertised names are always reputable, and usually there is a local cannery in your district that makes unheard-of but surprisingly delicious (and cheap) mushroom bisque or clam broth or tomato puree, according to the region you live in.

Once the cupboard is stocked with things you like and a few you are not sure about, start combining. [Or *adding!* Slices of ripe avocado on black bean soup, for instance, or fried cucumber slices in thin pea soup.] Put this and that together in a pan; stir them, heat them, and serve them as they are: tomato juice and clam juice, for instance.

Or add a dash of sherry at the last to cream of mushroom and tomato soup, or a flick of cinnamon or nutmeg over the top. Cream of pea and tomato soup are good with a little fresh-chopped basil. Chicken consommé and tomato juice are fine together, and even finer with a little lemon juice and a sprinkling of grated cheese at the last minute. A gout of sweet or sour cream is good in almost any clear soup, added at the last and stirred once or twice to make a swirl in the plate.

Or start at the beginning instead of the end, and stir a handful of chopped green onion into a little butter until wilted, and then pour tomato juice and beef bouillon into the pan, heat through, and serve with croutons made of little bread cubes fried in bacon until they are crisp and quite brown. These can be made in fairly large quantities and heated in the oven when they are needed, with a paper towel under them to collect the unnecessary fat.

It has been reported by fairly trustworthy travelers that natives along the Orinoco River in South America made a special kind of mudball for their soup, and think it a tasty tidbit indeed. Our present hemispheric policy of hands-across-borders forbids our murmuring anything but *¡Que deliciosa!* Here, in place of the clay-tinged delights of down yonder, we can make little balls of chopped raw beef mixed with fine herbs, roll them in flour to hold them together, and drop them into boiling beef and tomato consommé for five or ten minutes before serving.

Or we can buy a can of the excellent fishballs that are made in this country now instead of in Sweden, and put them, juice and all, into hot potato soup, with a goodly handful of chopped parsley to keep it all from looking too pale.

Or mix one egg and a scant cup of bread crumbs and about two tablespoons of grated cheese together. Add a little nutmeg, just to be reckless, and some salt and pepper. Have any kind of consommé you like boiling on the stove and then pour the mixture into it, beating like sixty-five all the time. Cover for about five minutes, beat again, and you have a shortcut Potage Mille Fanti, and very good too . . . probably. [Something average cooks do not do enough is use a liaison: an egg yolk or more, stirred in a little cream or stock and added just before serving to almost any kind of soup, to make it smoother, thicker, and more flavorful.]

Or put cooked rice or a little instant tapioca or a handful of the smallest kind of vermicelli into any thin soup you may have. (If you feel as I do about such pastes, and especially tapioca, you can pretend almost too easily as you eat it that you are back in a second-rate Swiss pension, watching three English women of advanced spinsterhood measure out their digestive tonic and trying not to listen to the Austrian honeymooners one table behind you. Even nostalgia is doubtful pleasure when evoked by limp globules of starch in the bouillon.)

Perhaps it would be better to call the whole thing off, that you should sink so low. Perhaps, rather than reach the point where you would willingly put tapioca in the soup, you should open the door, let the wolf prance in, and sigh, like the Southern lady, that you can't even boil water! [Unless . . . unless you can, thanks to a mad purchase or a generous uncle, make Consommé Talleyrand: Grate 4 large unpeeled truffles into a generous tureen. Add scant cup very dry sherry, 1 pinch cayenne. Cover and let stand one hour. Pour over it 3 pints hot rich consommé in which have been boiled 2 tablespoons tapioca. This is delicious.]

How to Greet the Spring

Young leaves everywhere;
The mountain cuckoo singing;
My first Bonito!
        Japanese haiku

For centuries people have believed that fish should be eaten (1) because it is a brain food and (2) because it is easily digested and (3) because it is bloodless and therefore suitable for religious fasts. Aside from these reasons, it has always been true that, in times of peace at least, fish is usually plentiful and more than usually good.

Now, however, with all the waters of the earth troubled and suspect, fish as a food has become a rarity. Even the gulls are starving, and the fishermen are fighting or in prison camps, and the people who once "had a kipper to their tea" . . . it is only to be wished for that they have found other adequate if less delectable substitutes. [From what I have heard, the exotics in English fish stalls, everything from whale to toheroa, were one of the heaviest crosses British cooks had to bear, during the long war (and "peace") years.]

In spite of the fact that many sea villages have lived for centuries on fish and bread and wine, there are wise biochemists who believe that fish as a food is harmful to the human system. This is truer of highly civilized cuisines than of the simple food in villages, but it is true everywhere that fish, like poultry, is a flesh that deteriorates rapidly unless it is kept very cold or mummified by smoking. At least one of these processes makes it harder to digest, just as baking the sensitive body of a hen's egg makes it tougher than leather in the human stomach.

War, then, which will fill all our refrigerated freight-carriers with other more vital cargoes, will make sea-fish as rare as dolphin's eggs, in the Middle West, and lake-fish something that children can read about in history books along the coasts.

The best way to have fish for supper, in most places, will be to go out along the river or in your dinghy at the tide's change, if you can get past sentries and avoid the mines, and catch some mudcats or a few bass on your own hook. The next best thing will be to eat some canned tuna or salmon, if you can still find a store that carries it . . . for the Italian fleet at San Francisco's Fisherman's Wharf is tied up now, and the canneries along the coast are waiting for other men to take the place of all the Japanese who used to work so neatly, slashing off heads and pressing out guts and packing the bodies in straight lines.

"The better the fish the simpler should be its preparation," Sheila Hibben says, and if you can find a fresh fish to cook, her wise word is the first to remember. [I have developed a real respect for frozen fish, both in filets and, as currently with trout, entire.] If the fish is good at all, its flavor will emerge much more honestly if it be simply broiled rather than covered with an intricate and expensive sauce. The grill should always be hot, so that the fish will not stick and break when it is moved, and of course should be hottest for the smallest fish, so that with thick slices it will not burn the outside before the interior is done.

A fish, which is usually prepared by the merchant, should be washed, dried, and then oiled, before it is seasoned for the grill.

The same is true if it is to be broiled in a shallow casserole. There should be plenty of melted butter, preferably heated with lime or lemon juice in it; and that, in most cases, is the perfect sauce, without even the distraction of a few minced herbs. [I usually rub soy sauce on fish before I oil it, unless it is very fresh and delicate indeed and especially if it is frozen. This adds a good taste to the final sauce. I buy soy sauce by the quart, but it might as well be the gallon, from a Korean-American called Paul.]

One of the great troubles about most fried fish in America (that is, *honest* fried fish, and not the sickening batter-coated monstrosity often sold in even reputable restaurants), is that it is overdone. Fish, like eggs, should be cooked quickly and lightly, and served at once in its own odorous heat.

The kind of fat you use for frying depends on your habits and your purse. Perhaps you believe that unsalted butter is the only proper medium, and that it should be poured away as soon as the fish is brown and more should be melted and poured over the dish. Perhaps you believe that a little bacon fat is a mighty fine thing, even for fresh trout, and that it's good not only on the fish but on some toast to eat alongside. The two schools of thought might be called *Haute Cuisine* and Campfire. There is no arguing with either, as long as the fish is fresh and the fat is honest. [I used to stand in line for catfish sent down from the Sacramento River, and the New Orleans girl named Bea who was helping me cook then would dip them lightly in white cornmeal that was quite heavily seasoned with *cayenne pepper*, before she fried them in good bacon grease. This may be a common trick, but I do not know of it. It works miracles.]

Any reputable cookbook holds many good recipes for preparing various kinds of fish, and such books as Mrs. Hibben's *Kitchen Manual* and Escoffier's American edition of the *Fine Art of Cookery* contain admirable discussions of the subject. [And I consider Brillat-Savarin's discussion of "The Art of Frying," in

The Physiology of Taste, necessary to any literate cook's background.] And if you get tired of the whole thing, you can slice almost any fine-grained fish in thin pieces, cover them with lemon or lime juice, and find them cooked in four hours without aid of stove or fire. They make a good hors d'œuvre, drained and coated lightly with a peppery mayonnaise.

In spite of some hidebound gastronomic judges who believe that any fish from a tin is fit only for alley cats, modern canned tuna and salmon and shrimps are a sensible addition to your menus, if you can get them. Indeed, you are probably safe to use any tinned fish you find, given, of course, that the tin itself is intact. [Cans grow surer all the time. One that looks puffed, and sends out a wheeze or whiff when pierced, should be discarded without cavil. Black insides are most often highly suspect too. And I rely mostly upon my Curious Nose. But in general modern canning is almost as dependable as those other two omnipresent realities, Death and Taxes.]

There are countless economical ways to prepare canned fish, and most of them take so little time that they are especially sensible for you if you work in a factory or an office.

Remember that the odor and flavor of the packed fish will be stronger than that of a fresh kind, and season your dish accordingly higher. Canned fish is already cooked, so need be heated only long enough to cook the other ingredients and blend the various flavors. It breaks easily, so should be added last to any sauce that needs stirring. The liquid that comes in the can is good, used in the same dish if possible. If it is an oil (which is increasingly unlikely), it is good in French dressing, for a change.

A nice Spanish recipe, which is easy and quick to make, is good with potatoes which have been peeled, diced, boiled quickly, and shaken with a handful of minced herbs and some butter.

Salmon (or Tuna) Pancake

2 *eggs*	1 *tablespoon minced parsley*
1 *cup canned salmon*	2 *tablespoons melted butter or oil*

Beat eggs, shred salmon, mix lightly, and add parsley. Form into a thick pancake, making solider with dried crumbs if necessary, and fry golden brown in the butter.

A recipe rather like this is from Hawaii, by way of China probably. It is a whole meal, and a good one too, with light beer or white wine to keep it company and perhaps a lime-and-pineapple ice afterward, if it is summer and you feel festive.

Hawaiian Shrimps

3 *tablespoons fat*	1 *small minced onion*
2 *cups tinned or fresh shrimps*	3 *tablespoons soy sauce*
½ *cup minced celery*	3 *cups cooked rice*
½ *cup chopped green pepper*	3 *eggs*
½ *cup chopped tinned or fresh mushrooms*	3 *tablespoons water*

Lightly brown onion in fat. Add celery, pepper, mushrooms, and cook 2 minutes.

Add shrimps, and turn lightly for 2 minutes. Then add the rice and soy (or Worcestershire) sauce [If you use Worcestershire, make it one tablespoon, of course. Soy sauce is salty, not peppery, as is the other.] and turn until hot, or about 2 minutes.

Stir the water and eggs together, and pour into the mixture. Stir all together quickly, and serve at once.

Another delicious shrimp dish, which is called a curry, although it has small resemblance to the real thing, is delicious with a plain green salad to follow, and then coffee.

Shrimp and Egg Curry

2	teaspoons curry powder (according to taste)	4	hard-cooked eggs, sliced hot fluffy rice
⅔	cup light cream		curry accompaniments:
2	cans condensed cream of mushroom soup		coconut, chutney, candied ginger, etc.
1½	cups shrimp (cooked, canned, or frozen)		

Blend the curry powder and cream. Add to the soup, and mix well. Add the shrimp and eggs, and heat over hot water, stirring as little as possible. Serve with hot rice and the accompaniments of any curry. This is well-adapted to chafing-dish cookery and is good for buffet suppers.

Condensed mushroom soup, while far from perfection, is a very present help in time of culinary trouble, and has made many a Queen Anne dish out of a Mary Anne base. The following recipe is typical of many such, and can be varied according to the herbs and ideas you possess:

Baked Tuna (or Salmon) with Mushroom Sauce

1	large can of fish salt and pepper	1	can of condensed cream of mushroom soup
1	sweet onion, sliced in thin rings	½	can of water
1	green pepper, cut in thin strips	2	teaspoons minced parsley grated cheese (optional)

Butter a baking dish generously, and make layers in it of the flaked fish, onion, pepper, and parsley. Dilute the soup with the water, and pour over all. Put grated cheese on top if desired. Bake about 20 minutes in a moderately hot oven (400°).

Of course, any such dish can be made in small casseroles, which take less time to bake. [Or in generous shells. I find most natural shells too small . . . like most sherry glasses . . . like most Gibson glasses . . . especially like most champagne glasses.] Canned mushrooms can be added, or sliced pimiento, or left-over peas . . . on and on.

It is a pity, in spite of biochemists who believe that we are better off without fish inside us, that war has interfered with our contrary tastes. The thought of all the bewildered sturgeons and barracudas dodging depth bombs is a sad one, as is the end of that wistful little Japanese who wrote so tenderly of the first succulent taste of bonito in the spring.

How Not to Boil an Egg

Hard-boiled, unbroken egg, what can you care
For the unfolded passion of the Rose?
H. P. PUTNAM

Probably one of the most private things in the world is an egg until it is broken.

Until then, you would think its secrets are its own, hidden behind the impassive beautiful curvings of its shell, white or brown or speckled. It emerges full-formed, almost painlessly [The *egg* may not be bothered, but nine years and two daughters after writing this I wonder somewhat more about the *hen*. I wrote, perhaps, too glibly.] from the hen. It lies without thought in the straw, and unless there is a thunderstorm or a sharp rise in temperature it stays fresh enough to please the human palate for several days.

In spite of the complete impersonality of its shell, however, some things about an egg can be guessed. People who know how can decide several rather surprising facts about it by holding it before a strong light, and even a zany will tell you that if it is none too fresh it will stand up and perhaps bob a little in a bowl of water.

The best thing to do with aged eggs is not to buy them, since they are fit for nothing, and a poor economy. If you find yourself the owner of a few, change your merchant with no more ado.

Hens, as long as they can find enough to eat, go right along at their chosen profession whether the country is at war or not, but unfortunately the product of all their industry is so delicate and perishable that when most of the fast trucks of the land are being used to shift soldiers here and there, the price of eggs goes much too high for comfort, whether or not the supply is good [. . . and so does the cost as well as the procurability of their feed].

During the last war housewives used to buy several dozen eggs when they were cheapest, and cover them in a crock with a singularly unpleasant stuff called water glass.

I can remember going down to the cellar and fishing around in the stone jar for two eggs for a cake the cook was making: the jellied chemical made a sucking noise as I spooned out the thickly coated hideous stuff, and I felt squeamish and afraid, alone there in the cool dark room. I decided then, and I still hold to it, that I would rather eat a good fresh egg only occasionally than have a whole cellarful of these dishonest old ones, which in spite of being "almost as good as new" would not make omelets, even, but had to be used in cakes and cookies.

Of course, the finest way to know that the egg you plan to eat is a fresh one is to own the hen that makes it. This scheme has many drawbacks, and I for one, as a person who has never felt any bond of sympathy between myself and a chicken[1] (their heads are too small, somehow, for their stupid, scratching, om-

---

[1] I think this should have an S on it: alive rather than prone upon a plate. I could happily forgo that too, even when cooked with the divine touch . . . or mushrooms.

nivorous bodies), have always been content to let someone else tend to the henhouse, even if I had to buy the product at much more than it would cost me to own one myself.

Eggs are a good investment now and then, expensive or not, and unless you are told otherwise by your doctor, or hate them in any form, they should be eaten in place of meat occasionally. The old-fashioned idea that they are "invalid food," something light and inconsequential, is fairly well proved foolish by the fact that two eggs are fully as nutritious as a juicy beefsteak . . . and ten times as hard to digest unless they are cooked with great wisdom.

Probably the wisest way to treat an egg is not to cook it at all. An accomplished barfly will prove to you that a Prairie Oyster [. . . as set forth on page 65] is one of the quickest pickups known to man, and whether you are hungover or merely tired, a raw egg beaten with a little milk or sherry can make you feel much more able to cope with yourself, and shortly too. [My children react happily to an egg yolk spread on dark bread and then well sprinkled with brown sugar, for a potent snack.]

A biochemist once told me that every minute an egg is cooked makes it take three hours longer to digest. The thought of a stomach pumping and grinding and laboring for some nine hours over an average three-minute egg is a wearisome one, if true, and makes memories of picnics and their accompanying deviled eggs seem actively haunting.

The simplest way to eat an egg, if you refuse to swallow it raw, even in its fanciest high-tasting disguises, is to boil it. Rather it is *not* to boil it, for no more erroneous phrase ever existed than "to boil an egg."

There are several ways *not* to boil an egg so that it will be tender, thoroughly cooked, and yet almost as easily digested as if it were raw.

One fairly good one is to drop the egg gently into simmering water, first running cold water over it so that it will not crack, and then let it stand there in the gentle heat for whatever time you wish. It will cook just as fast as if the water were hopping about in great bubbles, and it will be a better-treated egg, once opened.

Another way, which I think is the best one, is to cover the egg with cold water in a little pan. Heat it briskly, and as soon as it begins to bubble, the egg is done. It will be tenderer than when started in hot water, which of course makes the part nearest the shell cook immediately, instead of heating the whole thing gently.

I have never yet seen an egg crack when started in cool water, but some people automatically make a pinhole in every egg they boil, to prevent possible leaks, lesions, and losses.

(If you still want hard-boiled eggs, after pondering the number of hours, or days, it would take to digest them according to the biochemist, start them in cold water, turn the heat off as soon as it begins to bubble, and let them stand in it until it is cold. They will be tender, and comparatively free from nightmares.) [This is not as good a system as it is cracked up to be, to make a timid little pun. More often than not, I have found since I so optimistically wrote of it, the eggs do not peel properly. Half of the white comes off with the shell. Ho hum.]

If you think eggs boiled in their shells are fit food for the nursery, and refuse to admit any potential blessing in one delicately prepared, neatly spooned from its shell into a cup, sagely seasoned with salt and fresh-ground black pepper and a sizeable dollop of butter, all to be eaten with hot toast, then it is definitely not your dish. Instead, try heating a shallow skillet or fireproof dish, skirling a lump of butter [preferably waiting in the bottom, to absorb good melting heat from the egg . . .] or bacon grease or decent oil [This must have been a wartime aberration. Just lately I fired a cook who fried eggs in my best olive oil. The eggs, the oil, the whole house, and finally the cook took on an unbearable *slipperiness.*] in it until it looks very hot, and breaking a fresh egg or two into it. Then . . . and this is the trick . . . turn off the heat at once, cover the pan tightly, and wait for about three minutes. The result will be tender and firm, and very good indeed with toast and coffee, or with a salad and white wine for supper.

This method, of course, is a compromise. It is not a fried egg, strictly speaking, and yet it is as near to making a *good* fried egg as I have ever got.

I can make amazingly *bad* fried eggs, and in spite of what people tell me about this method and that, I continue to make amazingly bad fried eggs: tough, with edges like some kind of dirty starched lace, and a taste part sulphur and part singed newspaper. The best way to find a trustworthy method, I think, is to ask almost anyone but me. Or look in a cookbook. Or experiment.

There are as many different theories about making an omelet as there are people who like them, but in general, there are two main schools: the French, which uses eggs hardly stirred together, and the puffy or soufflé, which beats the white and yellow parts of the eggs separately, and then mixes them.

Then, of course, there is the Italian frittata school, which mixes all kinds of cooked cooled vegetables with eggs and merges them into a sort of pie; and a very good school that is.

Moreover, there is the Oriental school, best exemplified by what is usually called *foo yeung* in chop-suey parlors and is a kind of pancake of egg and bean-sprouts and and and.

To cap the whole thing, there is the school that has its own dependable and usually very simple method of putting eggs in a pan and having them come out as intended. Brillat-Savarin called them *oeufs brouillis* and I call them scrambled eggs.

The best definition of a perfect French omelet is given, perhaps unwittingly, in Escoffier's American translation of his *Guide Culinaire*: "Scrambled eggs enclosed in a coating of coagulated egg." This phrase in itself is none too appetizing, it seems to me, but it must do for want of a better man to say it. [This is said much more simply in its own language: *une omelette baveuse*.]

A French omelet worthy of the man, if not the definition, can be made, the second time at least if the first time it turns into a stiff ugly curd, by following these directions:

Basic French Omelet

6 *eggs*	*salt and pepper*
3 *tablespoons butter (good oil if absolutely necessary)*	

Be sure that the frying pan (8 or 10 inches) is smooth on the inside. Heat the butter in it until it gives off a nutty smell but does not brown. ("This will not only lend an exquisite taste," Escoffier says, "but the degree of heat reached in order to produce the aroma will be found to ensure the perfect setting of the eggs.") Roll the pan to cover the sides with butter.

Beat eggs lightly with a fork, add seasoning, and pour into pan. As soon as the edges are set, run a spatula under the center so that all the uncooked part will run under the cooked. [By now I know, fatalistically, that if I am using a pan I know, and if I have properly rolled the precise amount of sweet butter around that pan, and if the stars, winds, and general emotional climates are in both conjunction and harmony, I can make a perfect omelet without ever touching a spatula to it. Such occasions are historical, as well as accidental.] Do this once or twice, never leaving it to its own devices. When it is daintily browned on the bottom and creamy on top, fold it in the middle (or roll if you are a master), slide it onto a dish, and serve speedily.

Chopped herbs, cheese, mushrooms, and almost anything else may be added at your discretion, either at the first in the stirred eggs or when it is ready to fold. [Delicate creamed fowl or fish, generous in proportion to the size of each omelet, can be folded in, or new peas or asparagus tips, lightly cooked in butter.]

The second school of omelets is roughly defined as belonging to those addicts who believe eggs should be separated and then beaten hard, and then brought together again. Probably the main trick to remember in this technique is that the resulting foamy delicate mass should be cooked slowly instead of fast. [I don't know why I said this. It is true about scrambled eggs, surely, but a good omelet (soufflé) should be baked in a quick oven for fifteen to twenty minutes, or so I now firmly believe.] If this is done, it will "stand up firm and proud, instead of collapsing like a tired horse," says Mrs. Mazza. And she is right.

Basic Soufflé Omelet

6 *eggs*	5 *tablespoons hot water*
3 *tablespoons butter (or decent oil for want of better)*	*salt and pepper*

Separate eggs and beat whites until very stiff and yolks until creamy. Add the hot water and seasoning to the yolks, mix well, and fold in the whites. Heat a smooth skillet, add the butter, and roll it around the sides until it bubbles. Pour in the egg mixture, and leave over a very low fire until it is brown on the bottom. Place under the broiler to brown lightly on top. Test as for a cake with a toothpick, which should come out dry and clean when the omelet is done.

This omelet can be cut in two parts and any number of sauces of filling put between the layers and on top: Spanish sauce, chicken livers, leftover creamed sweetbreads, mushrooms in sherry . . . on and on.

Or try pouring a little rum over it and sprinkling it with powdered sugar, for a fine dessert. Or spreading it with chutney or any good preserve and grilling it again very quickly for a strange savory tailpiece to a meal. [Jeanne Bonamour in Dijon used to make cheese soufflés the way a good bartender mixes dry Gibsons, secure in a trance of habit and supreme self-confidence. She was careful to use moist fresh Swiss cheese and very fresh eggs (6), butter (4 tablespoons), and milk (1 cup). She mixed the milk and some flour in a small casserole . . . but her recipe is in any reputable collection of plain French cookery.]

An Italian frittata, which like all omelets is a fine dish for lunch or supper in any language, is a kind of pie or pancake filled with vegetables. It is made with olive oil instead of butter (if possible). Whatever odorous mulch of herbs and legumes that you make should be cooled and then added to the eggs.

Frittata of Zucchini
(For example)

3 tablespoons olive oil (or reputable substitute)	1 large fresh tomato or 1 cup solid-pack canned tomatoes
1 onion or three green onions	salt and pepper
1 clove garlic	1 teaspoon herbs . . . parsley, sweet marjoram, or thyme
5 small zucchini	9 eggs

Heat oil in skillet and cook minced onion and garlic slowly in it 10 minutes. Add zucchini cut into thin slices. Add peeled and cut-up tomato, seasoning, and herbs. Cover, and cook until the vegetable is tender. Take from stove and cool.

Beat eggs lightly, season, and mix with cooled vegetables. Pour back into skillet, cover tightly and cook over a slow fire until the edges of the frittata pull away from the pan. If the middle puffs up, prick it with a long sharp knife [. . . or better yet, pull away from sides once or twice with large spoon, to let the soft middle flow outward].

When it is solid, brown lightly under a slow broiler flame in a preheated oven, cut in slices like a pie, and serve at once.

This frittata is a good dish. It can be made with almost anything: string beans, peas, spinach, artichokes. Cheese can be sprinkled over it. [As an older and easily wiser frittata cook I almost always, these richer days, add a scant cup of good dry Parmesan cheese to the eggs when I mix them. Often I add rich cream, too. How easy it is to stray from austerity!] Different kinds of herbs like sweet basil, summer savory, on and on, can change its whole character. And with a glass of wine and some honest-to-God bread it is a meal. At the end of it you know that Fate cannot harm you, for you have dined.

Foo yeung is really another cut off the same loaf. The main difference between it and a frittata is that in the Oriental version the vegetables are diced and cooked only until they are crisply heated so that the whole texture is one of surprises, a mixture of sharp and soft, crisp and mellow, as all good Chinese dishes should be. This recipe can of course use gourmet powder (*mei jing*), [So many editors have shuddered away from my opinions on what we pompously call something like monoglutium sodomate that I'll only repeat here that it is a fine thing now and then, *but not all the time and in candy and coffee and on fresh green peas.*], diced roasted pork (*foo yuk*), diced peeled water chestnuts (*ma tai*), diced bamboo shoots (*jook tsun*), and a dozen other delicious things that are sold in Chinese stores. It can also be made without one of them and still taste as fresh and strange as any genuine Chinese omelet.

Basic Foo Yeung

4 eggs	½ cup celery
3 tablespoons good fat	½ cup green pepper
½ cup onion	½ cup mushroom

Brown chopped onion lightly in fat. Stir chopped or minced vegetables lightly into eggs. Let get firm and brown in pan, stirring up center once in a while. Cut into sections and serve quickly.

There are almost as many variations to this recipe as there are Chinese characters. Add shrimps. Add cooked rice. Add diced chicken. Add fried almonds [. . . or minced cooked porkhambeefvealfish]. Try mixing all the ingredients together and then frying in little cakes in the hot fat. It depends on whether you come from Canton, Changsha, or West Hollywood.

In between what I think are the most delicious eggs in the world and these other almost equally palatable concoctions with their exotic names—*frittata, soufflé aux fines herbes, gai foo yeung*—are a thousand dishes made from the fruit of the hen's expert if unconscious labor, and mixed according to your whim. Almost every good cook in the world has at least one ritual, usually histrionic, and more power to him! Here are three, fully guaranteed (although one of them is far from economical, and recommended only on state occasions, if the wolf seems definitely at the door).

Eggs In Hell
[*Uova in Purgatorio, Œufs d'en Bas, etc.*]

4 tablespoons olive oil (substitute will do, dad blast it)	1 teaspoon minced mixed herbs (basil, thyme)
1 clove garlic	1 teaspoon minced parsley salt and pepper
1 onion	8 eggs
2 cups tomato sauce (Italian kind is best, but even catsup will do if you cut down on spices)	slices of French bread, thin, toasted

Heat oil in a saucepan that has a tight cover. Split garlic lengthwise, run a toothpick through each half, and brown slowly in oil . . . Add the onion, minced, and cook until golden. Then add the tomato sauce and the seasonings and herbs. Cook about 15 minutes, stirring often, and then take out the garlic.

Into this sauce break the eggs. Spoon the sauce over them, cover closely, and cook very slowly until eggs are done, or about 15 minutes. (If the skillet is a heavy one, you can turn off the heat and cook in fifteen minutes with what is stored in the metal.)

When done, put the eggs carefully on the slices of dry toast, and cover with sauce. (Grated Parmesan cheese is good on this, if you can get any.)

There are too many variations of this recipe, even in my own mind, to be able to write. One I remember that we used to make, never earlier than two and never later than four in the morning, in a strange modernistic electric kitchen on the wine terraces between Lausanne and Montreux. We put cream and Worcestershire sauce into little casseroles, and heated them into bubbling. Then we broke eggs into them, turned off the current, and waited until they looked done, while we stood around drinking champagne with circles under our eyes and Viennese music in our heads. Then we ate the eggs with spoons, and went to bed.

A fair substitute for those faraway delightful shadows is what one young-painter-in-Mexico invented, called Eggs Obstaculos with nary a double entendre in any language:

Eggs Obstaculos

2	tablespoons butter or oil	8	eggs
¾	cup hot tomato sauce (salsa piquante) or ¾ cup tomato sauce and 8 drops tabasco sauce	1	cup beer hot toast

Heat oil and sauce in a shallow dish, rolling it well around the edges. When bubbling, break eggs into it. Heat slowly until the eggs are done, pour the beer over, and serve at once, with hot toast.

This recipe, like most good ones, has many variations, and unlike most of them, it is inexpensive if you have the ingredients at all.

It leads, by a somewhat crooked path, to what I think is the best way to cook eggs (unless you count hard-boiling them, cracking them on your own head, and eating them with salt and pepper and a glass of cold beer some hot summer day).

Scrambled eggs have been made, and massacred, for as long as people knew about pots and pans, no doubt. Very few know the rudiments held in this recipe now. I say it complacently, for I have tried it at least a hundred times, on people as various as a three-year-old Irishman and a poet laureate. (I have also tried to tell four cooks how to make it. Three of them were professionals and one was willing. All failed, I must add with somewhat less complacency.) [I am even less complacent than I was, having coped, like all honest cooks, with the uncountable quirks of eggs, and their unsuspected degrees of freshness and senescence. But I still feel that this recipe is superb, if you like very delicate creamy things now and then.]

Scrambled Eggs

(This dish is not very economical, but it is nourishing and pleasant enough for an occasional splurge.)

8 *good fresh eggs*	½ *pint rich cream . . . or more*

[. . . yes, good fresh eggs and rich cream . . . and yet I have produced something very good indeed with tired corner-store eggs and diluted condensed milk, given the time, which is, I am told, the essence.]

salt and freshly ground pepper	*grated cheese, herbs, whatnot, if desired*

Break eggs gently into cold iron skillet. Pour cream in, and stir quietly until the whole is blended, but no more. Never beat or whip. Heat very slowly, stirring from the middle bottom in large curds, as seldom as possible. Never let bubble. Add seasoning at the last stir or two.

This takes perhaps a half hour. It cannot be hurried.

Serve on toast, when it is barely firm. If herbs or cheese or mushrooms (or chicken livers and so forth) are added it should be when the eggs are half done.

It is a poor figure of a man who will say that eggs are fit only to be eaten at breakfast, served as they can be in these and countless other fashions. He himself may be as innocent as a new-laid egg, and unconscious of the manifold disguises, not to mention the artful invitations and devices, that can tempt him and the egg too. Let him ponder then, and if, wisely or not, he choose from all the possible forms an egg fresh-broken from the shell, cupped with a bit of lemon juice and pepper and any other seasoning to hand, and called an Oyster,[2] we can but hope that he has drunk well the night before and slept the sleep of the satisfied if not the just.

[2][The combination of one fresh raw unbeaten egg, one douse of Worcestershire sauce, one souse of whiskey or brandy, and one optional dibble of Tabasco-or-Evangeline-or-*salsa-piquante* (in that order of hellfire progression); it represents to many a jaded rounder the next morning's Last Resort. Not so to me. I often make one for myself before I must do something I dislike: go to the dentist, say. . . . I have been madly in love with mine, in a mild way, since I was nineteen, but I still need a Prairie Oyster to be able to stand going into his office.]

How to Keep Alive

Appetite, a universal wolf.
SHAKESPEARE

There are times when helpful hints about turning off the gas when not in use are foolish, because the gas has been turned off permanently, or until you can pay the bill. And you don't care about knowing the trick of keeping bread fresh by putting a cut apple in the box because you don't have any bread and certainly not an apple, cut or uncut. And there is no point in planning to save the juice from canned vegetables because they, and therefore their juices, do not exist.

In other words, the wolf has one paw wedged firmly into what looks like a widening crack in the door. Let us take it for granted that the situation, while uncomfortable, is definitely impermanent, and can be coped with.

The first thing to do, if you have absolutely no money, is to borrow some. Fifty cents will be enough, and should last you from three days to a week, depending on how luxurious are your tastes. [How grimly ridiculous *that* sounds, these days!] (Doctor Horace Fletcher, who believed that chewing food until it disappeared would help prevent senility, decayed teeth, stomachache, and several other equally tiresome phenomena, lived for years on eleven cents a day. And I know a man who spent two years at college on less than that, except that he cheated occasionally.)

As soon as you have procured fifty cents, find some kind soul who will let you use a stove, a food-grinder [any reasonable variation of what is now called a "food mill" is useful, for pureeing cooked vegetables and so on . . . unless that safe *chewed* texture is as unpleasant to you as to me. . . .] and a big kettle . . . the first for about three hours and the last for as long as you have any food. If you must pay for the stove, it will probably cost about ten cents for the current or gas. That cuts you down to forty cents.

You can either make a week's supply without meat, or about four days' with meat. Say you choose to be Lucullan: then buy about fifteen cents' worth of ground beef from a reputable butcher. (Be sure that it is beef and not what is none too euphoniously referred to as Hamburger.) This much meat will have few nourishing qualities, but it will make a good taste and its fat will stimulate you and help keep you warm. [Anywhere along here is all right for my heartfelt comment that this sounds both silly and disagreeable, but that basically it is a workable suggestion, given reasonable good sense and a certain amount of desperation, both of them dictated by the actual State of War . . . against either wolf or fellow man.]

Buy about ten cents' worth of ground whole-grain cereal. Almost any large grocery carries it in bulk. It is brownish in color, coarsely mealy in texture and has a pleasant smell of nuts and starch.

Spend the rest of your money on vegetables. Buy them if you can at a big market that most probably has a counter of slightly wilted or withered things a day old maybe. Otherwise buy the big coarse ugly ones in any store. If you know the merchant and he likes you, he will feel passionately interested in your well-being and will help you economize as if you were his own child, with mutual amusement.

Get one bunch of carrots, two onions, some celery, and either a small head of cabbage or the coarse outer leaves from some heads that should be trimmed a bit anyway. It does not matter if they be slightly battered: you will wash them and grind them into an odorous but unrecognizable sludge.

The other vegetables depend on how much money you have left and what the season or your will may be. Squashes, like zucchini, are good, and of course tomatoes. Beans are fine. There can hardly be too much celery, if you like it. A clove of garlic is highly to be recommended . . . *if* you like it. Turnips are too strong, and beets of course would make the whole thing into a ghoulish, ghastly, and completely horrendous mess of pink and cerise [. . . and finally gray]. Potatoes are useless; the cereal takes care of any need for starch, and bulk as well.

Assemble what vegetables you have. Grind them all into the pot. Break up the meat into the pot. Cover the thing with what seems too much water. Bring to a boil, let simmer about an hour, and stir in the ground grain-cereal. Mix thoroughly, and cook very slowly another two hours, or longer if possible. Let cool, and keep in a cold place (the cellar in summer if you have no icebox handy or borrowable).

You can eat it cold and not suffer much, if your needs are purely animal and unfinanced, but if you can heat what you want two or three times a day it will probably taste much better. (A little of it sliced and fried like scrapple is absolutely delicious, but of course, that takes it into the luxury class, what with the fat you'd need, and the fire.)

It is obvious to even the most optimistic that this sludge, which should be like stiff cold mush, and a rather unpleasant murky brown-gray in color, is strictly for hunger. [One way to make it prettier, gastronomically, is to brown the meat in a handful of flour, to a handsome walnut shade. Another is to use a douse of dear old Kitchen Bouquet, toward the end but while you can still stir it thoroughly into the aptly named Sludge.] It is functional, really: a streamlined answer to the pressing problem of how to exist the best possible way for the least amount of money. I know, from some experience, that it can be done on this formula, which holds enough vitamins and minerals and so on and so forth to keep a professional strongman or a dancer or even a college professor in good health and equable spirits.

The main trouble with it, as with any enforced and completely simple diet, is its monotony. It must be considered, then, as a means to an end, like ethyl gasoline, which can never give much esthetic satisfaction to its purchaser or the automobile it is meant for but is almost certain to make that automobile run smoothly.

"When food is not appetizing it lies in the stomach like lead," an American gastronomist named Henry Finck decided in 1913. The idea was not original with him but it is a good one, and makes it plainer than ever that this Down-with-the-Wolf formula could very easily lie like lead unless you really need it.

Then, if you had to choose between it and hunger, with its inevitable aftermath of fatigue and bad teeth and dull hair and wrinkles, you would eat it three times a day as long as the emergency lasted and perhaps even derive a certain esthetic satisfaction from your own good sense, if not from the food itself.

Other systems for living on little have been evolved, of course, and for a time at least have proved fairly successful. One mother of five growing children fed them and their father and herself, during what is still referred to as the Depression, on something like five dollars a month for five months. She went so far as to write a book about it, illustrated with a family photograph of what looked like slightly overweight but average people. [The fat look of some starving people is even more familiar now than in 1942, unhappily.]

I have occasionally thought of her and her system, and have wanted, in a faintly masochistic mood, to see what five years rather than five months of farinaceous vegetables and cheap spaghettis and breads would do to the teeth and innards of her brood. According to most nutritionists, the picture would not be so pretty. [One boy I know, who was adolescent during the thinnest months of Occupation in Burgundy, is now too tall and very listless. And a girl, adolescent now and a happy baby then, is much more bitterly ill-tempered and voracious than her age would justify.]

The man I know who lived for two years on about seven cents a day (this was in the early thirties at the University of California) was and still is a bonny figure indeed, tall, lean, and wholesome . . . physically at least. (Spiritually he is a disciple of Henry Miller, which in some people's eyes is a form of disease.) Perhaps an empty stomach is not a good literary adviser, to misquote Einstein's observation about hunger and politics. [I think the parenthetical and unsolicited cultural comment should close here and not above. It still stands, according to some critics.]

His formula was simple, but as I said before, he cheated now and then.

He would buy whole ground wheat at a feed-and-grain store, cook it slowly in a big kettle with a lot of water until it was tender, and eat it three times a day with a weekly gallon of milk that he got from a cut-rate dairy. Amost every day he stole a piece of fruit from a Chinese pushcart near his room. (After he graduated he sent the owner a ten-dollar bill, and got four dollars back, with an agreeable note inviting him to a New Year's party in Chinatown in San Francisco. He went.)

Every three weeks or so he had a job as waiter at fraternity-house banquets and other such collegiate orgies. He always took a basket and a rope, and let down into the alley sometime during the evening a surprising collection of rolls, butter, olives, pie, and even chicken or meat. After one or two sad experiences with alley cats, who found his basket before he got to it, he knew how to close it firmly against any marauders but himself, and would hurry back to his room with it as soon as the waiters were dismissed.

He confessed much later that the food never tasted good and that it was always a relief to get back to boiled wheat and milk again but that for two years he wolfed down those frowsy stolen scraps as if they were his one link with *la gourmandise*.

He was fortunate that his chosen way to keep alive agreed with his guts, if not completely with his gourmet instincts. The woman who fed her family cooked starch for five months was perhaps equally lucky; at least she kept them alive, which is supposed to mean heaven for true mothers. Myself, I shall choose my own peculiar brew of vegetables and meat and cereal if need be, for like the student and the mother and every other human, I feel that my own system is the best . . . until a better one occurs to me. [It has not yet done so. I believe more firmly than ever in fresh raw milk, freshly ground whole grains of cereal, and vegetables grown in organically cultured soil. If I must eat meats I want them carved from beasts nurtured on the plants from that same kind of soil. As for fish . . . they can choose their own way of life in my gastronomy, unless we interrupt it with split atoms.]

And to all of us I shall say, with wise Aesop, "You have put your head inside a wolf's mouth and taken it out again in safety. That ought to be reward enough for you."

How to Rise
Up Like New Bread

> "Lord Jesus Christ, have mercy and save me! Let me lie down like a stone, O God, and rise up like new bread," Platon prayed, and turning over, he fell asleep at once.
>
> *War and Peace,* TOLSTOY

For years you have had to be a voice crying in the wilderness [now comparatively crowded, thank God] to dare say anything against the mockery of our staff of life, and now, when war and perhaps a growing sensibility have made us think more of vitamins and their relation to poor teeth and jumpy nerves and such, we still condone the stupid bread in this country. [True, in spite of the optimistic note just above.]

Newspapers tell us, with government permission, that wheat costing some five cents a pound is "refined" until it is not only tasteless but almost worthless nutritionally, and that the wheat germ that is thus removed is then sold for at least a dollar and a half and at the end put back into the bread, so that in loaves it can be sold for a little more than the ordinary price and called "Super-Vitaminized" or "Energized" or some such thing.

The English Food Ministry has been trying ever since the second World War began to make its subjects buy whole-cereal breads rather than the emasculated pale stuff sold by every self-respecting bakery. Apparently class snobbism has conquered once more over good sense, for no matter what proof the Ministry gives that white bread will cause bad teeth, poor eyes, weak back, fatigue, the Britishers go on eating what has for decades meant refinement and "good taste," socially if not gastronomically. [In Switzerland, at least when I lived there, every bakery must make a daily batch of "federal formula bread," according to its total output. It always embarrassed François, my houseman, to have me buy the dark nutty moist stuff instead of gentler paler loaves.]

Here we are perhaps less stubborn, since we are made up of a lot of different nationalities mainly brought from the lower classes, and in almost any decent-sized village of our country there is a baker from Hungary or Poland or France who can and does still make his round odorous healthful loaves.

In every big city there is a good handful of restaurants, mostly kosher, that put flat baskets of various breads on every table, and the breads are so good, so dark and crusty and full of flavor, that the waiters have to hop to keep them filled, whether the diners be Jew or wandering Gentile.

And in spite of this, and what seems an inborn and growing hunger for decent bread, we continue everywhere to buy the packaged monstrosities that lie, all sliced and tasteless, on the bread-counters of the nation, and then spend money and more money on pills containing the vitamins that have been removed at great cost from the wheat. [Today, with a bakers' strike on, the only bread at my store came from a small Franco-Italian factory. It lay piled in fine unsliced unwrapped odorous loaves, and all the housewives looked blankly at it and asked, almost in tears, "But where's the *sandwich* bread?"]

It is a crying shame, for fair.

Lately, perhaps because of the very propaganda that seems so contradictory, it has been easier to buy bread with a little taste to it, once you have conquered your distrust of the thick neat slices and the transparent wrappings. You have even been able to get sourdough bread once a week in some groceries: a frail wisp of the old nose-tickling loaf, but at least an effort in the right direction.

It is hard, often, not to be impatient at our slowness. Sometimes, when you go past a little factory in the "foreign" section of a town, and smell the honest exciting smell of real bread baking, you remember a part of your childhood, and feel a child's helplessness before the fact of a whole nation's cautious acceptance of its own simplicity. It is difficult for us, after years of trying to be highfalutin and refined, to admit that plush drapes in the parlor and pale white bread are not our dish at all.

Perhaps this war will make it simpler for us to go back to some of the old ways we knew before we came over to this land and made the Big Money. Perhaps, even, we will remember how to make good bread again.

It does not cost much. [It costs more than ordinary chain-store stuff. But it is a sound investment, at least now and then.] It is pleasant: one of those almost hypnotic businesses, like a dance from some ancient ceremony. It leaves you filled with peace, and the house filled with one of the world's sweetest smells. But it takes a lot of time. If you can find that, the rest is easy. And if you cannot rightly find it, make it, for probably there is no chiropractic treatment, no Yoga exercise, no hour of meditation in a music-throbbing chapel, that will leave you emptier of bad thoughts than this homely ceremony of making bread.

You should have four bread pans, which can be bought usually at a junk-man's if one of your female relatives does not have them stuck away in some cupboard under the back stairs. [I had four of my maternal grandmother's: a good friend quietly liberated two, and an enemy the rest. I still have Grandmother's black cast-iron "gem-tins," and *I plan to keep them.* I haven't made a popover for years, but when I do I'll need those "tins" and no others.] You might even buy the glass ones, which are very good, although less romantic. You will need a big bowl, too.

Given these props, then, and an oven that will hold the four pans, you can safely embark on what may, for the first time at least, be a harrowingly entertaining experience, but will probably lead to many calmer, peace-bringing times.

White Bread

4	cups (1 quart) milk	1	cake compressed yeast, or 1
¼	cup sugar		package dry granular yeast
4	teaspoons salt	¼	cup lukewarm water
2	tablespoons shortening	12	cups sifted all-purpose flour
			(approximately)

From there on, when you first assemble the ingredients, the dance begins. It is one that should be rehearsed a few times, probably, but I know that it can be done with astonishing if somewhat frenzied smoothness the first time.

First scald the milk. Then add the sugar, salt, and shortening, and let the whole cool until it is lukewarm. Then add the yeast, which has been softened in the tepid water.

Start stirring in the flour, mixing it slowly and thoroughly. When the dough is stiff enough to be handled easily, turn it out onto a lightly floured board or tabletop, and knead it until it is smooth and satiny.

Kneading bread means pressing it rhythmically with the heel and fingers of each hand, in a gentle rocking movement, turning the dough over on itself with each push, folding it lightly, pushing, pressing. It is a calming, musical rhythm. In 8 or 10 minutes, when the dough looks and feels as smooth as silk, you can stop.

Then shape the kneaded dough into a smooth ball, and place it in a bowl that has been lightly greased. [Fresh unsalted butter or virgin peanut oil I like best, whenever I indicate grease or fat. But according to the uses of the bread, anything good can be used, from bacon drippings to goose-schmaltz.] Brush the surface fleetingly with melted fat, cover with a lid or a heavy cloth, and let rise in a warm place until it has doubled in bulk. Overnight is easiest. If you press the dough gently with your finger and a hole stays there, it is light enough.

Punch with your folded fist into the soft white mound, down as far as you can go. Then fold the edges into the hole you have made, turn the ball smooth side up, and cover and let it rise again.

When it is light enough to hold the impression of your finger, punch into it again. Then divide the dough into four even parts with a sharp knife, and round each part lightly into a smooth ball. Cover them well, and let stay tranquil for about fifteen minutes.

Mold each one, then, into a loaf, by flattening it, and folding and stretching and rolling and stretching and folding until it will fit lightly into a greased pan, with the last seam on the bottom and a firm smooth top where it should be. [A temporarily retired lieutenant-colonel with jitters calmed himself by baking for his friends, and evolved a flattish tough wonderful loaf we all called Old Testament, made of stoneground flours. He put about three of them onto a big cookie sheet. They were truly Biblical, and made clearer the significance of "breaking bread."]

Brush the tops with melted fat, and let rise in a warm place until they have doubled in bulk. And then bake in a moderately hot oven (400 to 425°) for 40 to 45 minutes.

When the loaves are golden, slip them from their pans onto racks of any kind, to cool.

You can stand and look at them, even the first time, with an almost mystical pride and feeling of self-pleasure. You will know, as you smell them and remember the strange cool solidity of the dough puffing up around your wrist when you hit it, what people have known for centuries about the sanctity of bread. You will understand why certain simple men, in old centuries, used to apologize to the family loaf if by accident they dropped it from the table.

There is another recipe for a good bread, which will interest you perhaps enough to try, once you have proved at least your armchair wings with the first one:

Hot Loaf

1	pint milk	1	cake yeast
1	boiled potato	1	teaspoon salt
1½	tablespoons lard		flour
1	tablespoon sugar		

Mash the potato and beat until light. After the milk is brought to a boil, add the potato, lard, and sugar and salt. When the mixture is lukewarm, add the yeast which has been dissolved in a little of the potato water.

Sift in enough flour to make the dough soft and workable. Then knead well, place in a large bowl, and set in a warm room to rise overnight.

Next morning turn the dough out onto a floured board and knead 2 or 3 minutes. Form into a round loaf, and place in a greased lard bucket. Let rise for two hours, and bake in a moderate oven until a fine golden crust is formed.

This rather quaint rule is from an old Virginian cookbook, and I for one am quite ignorant of what a lard bucket looks like. It reminds me of what a Frenchman once told me, though, about the bread that was baked in his home when he was little. It was always put into clean clay flowerpots, he said! It has a fresh sweet flavor that no other bread could ever have . . . and "Try it," he said. "You will see! You can make tiny loaves for each person, and the clean washed clay will change your bread as you never thought manmade thing could dare to!" [I almost lost a dear friend with this trick: apparently she was too sparing with the butter on the clay, or the clay was not wet enough to begin with. . . . The loaves stuck. She has since forgiven me and brings me fresh warm bread wrapped, as it should be, in a clean tattered linen napkin.]

And here is the recipe for:

Addie's Quick Bucket-Bread

1 *cake fresh yeast*	1½ *tablespoons salt*
1 *cup lukewarm water*	3 *tablespoons sugar*
3 *tablespoons shortening*	10 *to* 12 *cups all-purpose flour*
1 *quart whole rich milk*	*grease, butter*

Dissolve the yeast in the water. Melt the shortening in the milk, but do not let it boil. Combine the two liquid mixtures in a big bowl. Into another big bowl or kettle sift the blended salt, sugar, and flour. Pour the liquid gradually into the flour, mixing well, and when feasible knead until smooth. Put the dough into a heavily greased pan, cover with a clean napkin or towel, and let stand in a warm place until double in size. Knead lightly, and let rise once more (about 3½ hours altogether). Make into loaves (Addie slashes her dough into pieces with a sharp knife and then slaps it into shape as if it were a Bad Boy . . . but any good recipe gives as logical, if less lusty, a procedure), put into well-greased pans, and bake at 350° for about 1 hour. Brush butter on the tops when once they start to brown, and again when the loaves are removed from their pans.

This bread is fine in regular pans, but Addie uses two- (or one- or three-) pound coffee-tins. A ball of dough at the bottom of one will make a loaf about four times as high, a delightful slightly buttery light odorous thing, fine for toast, sandwiches, eggs poached or pseudo-Benedict or or or. . . . Children love its roundness.

And aside from the quaint practicability of the pans the recipe is valuable, I think, because it makes excellent bread in a much shorter time than most cooks will grant is possible.

But whether it be flowerpots or modern glass or old Southern lard bucket, or even coffee-tins, there are always containers for the bread to rise and bake in. Why is that? Why can you not make the kind of round loaf, perhaps with a cross slashed on the top of it, that you used to see through a cellar door when you walked home from the theater late at night in France? The white-faced baker's boy, with flour in his eyebrows and his pores and probably his lungs, slid it surely, intensely, on a long shovel into the blaze of the open oven. It was naked, like a firm-hipped woman, without benefit of metal girdlings. It came out, in an hour or so, ready for next morning's breakfast, round and brownly even and filled with an honorable savor. It was good bread, and you can make it.

You can forget the soggy sterile slices that pop up dourly in three million automatic toasters every morning. [Why do I say three, either then or now? I own one myself, which makes it at least three million and one, and I hate everything about it, except a rare slice of bread that seems in conjunction with the workings of the robot within, and springs up rightly golden, rightly crisp.] and instead cut for yourself, if you will, a slice of bread that you have seen mysteriously rise and redouble and fall and fold under your hands. It will smell better, and taste better, than you remembered anything could possibly taste or smell, and it will make you feel, for a time at least, newborn into a better world than this one often seems.

How to Be
Cheerful Though Starving

Obsession by economic issues is as local and transitory as it is repulsive and disturbing.

The Acquisitive Society, RICHARD HENRY TAWNEY

When you are really hungry, a meal eaten by yourself is not so much an event as the automatic carrying out of a physical function: you must do it to live. [I now disagree completely with this, and could and probably will write a whole book proving my present point, that solitary dining, no matter what the degree of hunger, can be good.] But when you share it with another human or two, or even a respected animal, it becomes dignified. Suddenly it takes on part of the ancient religious solemnity of the Breaking of Bread, the Sharing of Salt. No matter what your hunger nor how fiercely your fingers itch for the warmness of the food, the fact that you are not alone makes flavors clearer and a certain philosophic slowness possible.

And it is well to eat slowly: the food seems to be more plentiful, probably because it lasts longer.

There are many ways to make a little seem like more. They have been followed and changed and reinvented for ten thousand years, with small loss of dignity to mankind. Indeed, sometimes their very following is a thing of admiration, because of the people who are poor and who refuse to be obsessed by that fact until it becomes "repulsive and disturbing."

Of course, it takes a certain amount of native wit to cope gracefully with the problem of having the wolf camp with apparent permanency on your doorstep. That can be a wearing thing, and even the pretense of ignoring his presence has a kind of dangerous monotony about it.

For the average wolf-dodger, good health is probably one of the most important foils. Nothing seems particularly grim if your head is clear and your teeth are clean [Toothpaste now contains chlorophyl. Animals still chew grass.] and your bowels function properly.

Another thing that makes daily, hourly thought about wherewithals endurable is to be able to share it with someone else. That does not mean, and I say it emphatically, sharing the fuss and bother and fretting. It means being companionable with another human who understands, perhaps without any talking at all, what problems of basic nourishment confront you. [This still obtains, as my legal friends say. It is the condition most devoutly to be wished for. However, the years have taught me compromises, as they have all thinking creatures.] Once such a relationship is established, your black thoughts vanish, and how to make a pot of stew last three more meals seems less a nightmare than a form of sensual entertainment.

There was one person, though, who was a part of my education and who refuted all my tentative rules for fortunate wolf-dodging, and did it with such grace that I often think of her half-doubtingly, as if she were a dream.

Her name was Sue. She was delicate bodily . . . not ill, but never well the way most people are well. She flitted like a night moth through all her days, bemazed by the ardors of sunlight but conducting herself with wary sureness, so that she seldom banged against shut doors or hit her thin bones on sharp table corners.

She was, as far as anyone knew, completely alone. It was impossible to think of her in any more passionate contact with other humans than the occasional suppers she gave for them. The fact that once she must have been young did not change her present remoteness: you could not see her any warmer at seventeen that at seventy.

But her withdrawn impersonal attitude did not make her any less delicately robust. She loved to eat, and she apparently loved, now and then, to eat with other people. Her suppers were legendary. Of course, it depended on who was telling about them: sometimes they were merely strange, or even laughable, and sometimes they sounded like something from a Southern California Twelfth Night, with strange games and witchlike feastings.

Sue lived in a little weatherbeaten house on a big weatherbeaten cliff. At first when you entered it, the house seemed almost empty, but soon you realized that like all dwellings of old lonely people, it was stuffed with a thousand relics of the fuller years. There were incredibly dingy and lump-filled cushions that Whistler had sat on, and a Phyfe chair that had one stormy night been kicked into kindling wood by Oscar Wilde. It was held together with rubber bands, and naturally was not to be used as a chair, but rather as a casually treated but important altar.

When you went to her house, you ate by one candle, no matter whether you were two or eight at table. Of course this seemed intensely romantic to young Americans, but it was because she could afford neither more candles nor electricity.

The walls, covered with third-rate etchings by first-rate men, and a few first-rate ones by the almost unknown Sue, emerged gradually from the dingy darkness. There was an underlying smell, delicate as early death, of age and decay.

The main smell, though, was a good one. It never had the forthright energy of braised meat (although I remember one time, when I may have looked a little peaked, that Sue went against her custom and put a tiny morsel of cooked liver on my plate, and said, "Now, I want you to try to eat *all* of this!" It was no bigger than a dollar, and I made it into at least twelve bites, in a kind of awe).

There was always the exciting, mysterious perfume of bruised herbs, plucked fresh and cool from the tangle of weeds around the shack. Sue put them into a salad.

Then there was usually sage, which she used like a Turk or Armenian in practically everything that went into her pot. She gathered it in the hills, and dried it in bunches above her stove, and in spite of gastronomical scouts who wail now that California sage all has a taste of turpentine, hers never did. She knew only about a hundred kinds, she confessed quietly; someone had told her that the hills behind the village held at least fifty more.

Sue had only a few plates, and no knives. You ate everything from one large Spode soup-plate, when you went there, but it never seemed mussy. And knives were unnecessary, because there was nothing to cut.

As I remember now, her whole cuisine was Oriental. There were the little bowls of chopped fresh and cooked leaves. There were the fresh and dried herbs, which she had gathered from the fields. There was the common bowl of rice (or potatoes that Sue had probably stolen the night before from some patch up the canyon). There was tea, always. There was, occasionally, a fresh egg, which also was stolen, no doubt, and which Sue always put in the teapot to heat through and then broke over the biggest dish of food.

I have never eaten such strange things as there in her dark smelly room, with the waves roaring at the foot of the cliff and Whistler's maroon-taffeta pillow bruising its soft way into the small of my back. People said that Sue robbed garbage pails at night. She did not, of course. But she did flit about, picking leaves from other gardens than her own and wandering like the Lolly Willowes of Laguna along the cliff-tops and the beaches looking in the night light for sea-spinach and pink ice-plant. [For long now the cliffs have been covered with villas, and the wild herbs have vanished. I still taste and smell them in my memory, and feel the close-packed cold beads of the ice-plant's leaves and petals.]

The salads and stews she made from these little shy weeds were indeed peculiar, but she blended and cooked them so skillfully that they never lost their fresh salt crispness. She put them together with thought and gratitude, and never seemed to realize that her cuisine was one of intense romantic strangeness to everyone but herself. I doubt if she spent more than fifty dollars a year on what she and her entranced guests ate, but from the gracious abstracted way she gave you a soup dish full of sliced cactus leaves and lemon-berries and dried crumbled kelp, it might as well have been stuffed ortolans. Moreover, it was good.

I doubt very much if anybody but Sue could make it good. Few other humans know the secret of herbs as she did . . . or if they know them, can use them so nonchalantly.

But anyone in the world, with intelligence and spirit and the knowledge that it must be done, can live with her inspired oblivion to the ugliness of poverty. It is not that she wandered at night hunting for leaves and berries; it is that she cared enough to invite her friends to share them with her, and could serve them, to herself alone or to a dozen guests, with the sureness that she was right.

Sue had neither health nor companionship to comfort her and warm her, but she nourished herself and many other people for many years, with the quiet assumption [this is very important] that man's need for food is not a grim obsession, repulsive, disturbing, but a dignified and even enjoyable function. Her nourishment was of more than the flesh, not because of its strangeness, but because of her own calm. [And this, too, is very important.]

How to Carve the Wolf

Meat puddings should be served between the months of
September and April; during the months without an "R" in
them meat pies should replace them.

LE VICOMTE DE MAUDUIT

[It is unflattering but fortunate that nobody has ever asked me
the difference between a meat pie and a meat pudding. Do I
really know?]

I

For several years before France fell, Paris newspapers as different as *Le Temps* and *L'Intransigeant* ran irate and direful letters
from old-fashioned chefs predicting that sure as shooting
something awful would happen to the whole country unless the
young people forgot their new fad for sports and grilled steak-
with-watercress and went back intelligently to the rich *cuisine
des sauces* of their fathers.

Not only was this shocking appetite driving the chefs themselves to the poorhouse, but it was un-French. It bespoke a crass
lack of national spirit, a betrayal of all that was best in the Gallic
culture, to order a Chateaubriand (*saignant*) in a decent restaurant, when one could as easily command a little pigeon simmered artfully with red wine and truffles and this and that and
mushrooms maybe . . . and many spices . . . and one or two

kinds of fat . . . and probably a little basting of marc or brandy at the last.

What the chefs would say now, if they could, can never be known. The young girls and men who ate grilled steak in their sport clothes at the Café de Paris are as much a secret as the Café de Paris itself. Ghosts of the great restaurants and their cooks may cry that lack of spirit and finesse betrayed the old as well as the unborn; ghosts of the young may answer that richness and subtlety were but a kind of phosphorescence on the decayed culture that Carême and Vatel and all the other masters left to them.

Ghosts are not worried by wolves. The psychological effects of grilled or besauced beef on a nation's temperament cannot matter much to clay, or so we prefer to think. [When I am cook for the carnivorous, my true salute to them is a beef filet, of about four pounds. I turn it for at least three hours in a garlicky marinade, half olive oil, half soy sauce. I roast it on a rack for one-half hour in a very hot oven. I slice it one-inch thick, slip generous wedges of maître-d'hotel butter between each slice, pour a good cup of red wine over the whole, and serve it in its various hot juices. Even ghosts . . .] But to the living, who must eat to stay so, beef in any form is a problem indeed.

There are several more or less logical reasons why meat grows scarce in wartime: soldiers need it, there are fewer cattle, zub zub zub. It is unfortunate that so many human beings depend on eating some form of animal flesh every day for strength. Many of them do it because their bodies, weakened or diseased, demand it. Others simply have the habit. Habit or necessity, it becomes a truly worrisome expense in wartime, so that money spent for meat must be used to buy as much nourishment as possible, even at the risk of a certain monotony.

The old idea that if you boil even a useless piece of meat long enough you will extract all its juices, which then form a fine stimulating nutritive broth, is looked on with suspicion by most modern food-experts [. . . including Brillat-Savarin, who died in 1825, only a few years ago]. They say that by the time you drink the juices, they are so dead that they are useless to any human organism. Instead, the experts advise, the quickest and easiest way to absorb all the minerals and vitamins present in a piece of meat is to chop it finely and eat it raw.

This brutal simplification should make the ghosts of the Paris chefs wail even louder, and itch to write another letter to *L'Intransigeant*. But I remember several times in their city, living then, when I was tired and wanted a quick pickup (or when I had eaten one too many of their artful sauces), that they made Bœuf Tartare for me. Of course, they elaborated it as much as possible, and each time it was a little different, like a good Indian curry, but this is the basis:

Bœuf Tartare

¼ pound beef per person (or more)	olive oil
1 egg per person	parsley, chives, basil, any herbs
lemon juice	salt, pepper

Remove all fat from meat and grind rather coarse. Form lightly into mounds or pats, 1 for each person. Make a little dent on the top.

Break the eggs carefully, saving the whites for another purpose, and put a yolk in a half-shell in the dent on each pat.

Chop the herbs separately and put into little bowls. Serve the olive oil in a cruet. Garnish the meat with lemon-quarters. Other things like little pickled onions and chopped dill pickles and so forth may be added to the tray.

To eat, put the egg-yolk into the dent, cover the whole with whatever herbs desired, add olive oil and lemon juice and seasoning, and mix lightly.

This somewhat barbaric dish is best with crisp bread and a glass of fairly plain red wine. It is quickly digested and leaves a pleasant feeling on the palate, if you can swallow it at all, which some people would rather starve than do [. . . or if you can keep it from the eager exhibitionism of the waiter, who pants to turn it into a gastronomical proof that gray can be made with even a few too many colors (or flavors) mixed together].

The distinction between raw and rare is a subtle one, only to be settled in the individual mind. Many a person who could not even think of eating Bœuf Tartare without gagging (unfortunately, because it can be made of inexpensive and often highly nutritive cuts of beef), would willingly assault a thick bloody lukewarm "cut off the joint" and feel himself secure in the tradition of Simpson's and the Plaza and Dave Chasen's . . . and Henry the Eighth's own dining hall, as far as that goes.

There is no doubt about it, a handsome roast *is* handsome, and probably the most satisfying meat to the average Anglo-Saxon hunger. It grows increasingly scarce and relatively priceless.

Nevertheless, it is a wise extravagance now and then if it can be had at all, since for the average family it will make several meals, and only the first cooking uses much fuel. (There will be cold roast beef with salad, and then sandwiches, and then perhaps Bœuf Moreno or some such concoction, and then maybe hash [A hash can be very fine indeed. The worst thing that can happen to it is a grinder; everything that is choppable in it should be *chopped*.] or even a curry, or croquettes if you can afford a "frying kettle" and approve of these synthetic pyramids . . . on and on . . . or maybe it disappears practically at once! In this case you had better not buy it again for a long time, unless your rich godfather dies.

There are two definite ways to start to roast beef, or any

meat. For the last few years the government experts have urged that women put the meat into an oven of 300 degrees, at which temperature it remains for an average of twenty minutes per pound. The loss by shrinkage is practically erased, and the flavor of the meat, it is said, is much better. The meat browns gradually, until by the time it is done, it is as beautiful as it should be.

The older school disagrees thoroughly with this system, and at least has custom on its side, if not economy. It holds that the first twenty-five minutes of a roast's final death are the most important. They should be spent at a temperature of about 500 degrees, so that the whole surface is seared and all the juices are sealed into the meat. After that, the oven heat is reduced to about 300 degrees, as in the other process. [The proof of the roasting is the taste therefrom, and certainly the new system tastes best to me, in the face of my recognized masters.]

Aside from the first temperature, the way to roast a good cut of beef, preferably one with about two ribs in it, is the same. The meat is wiped carefully with a damp cloth or a cut lemon, and then rubbed with salt and pepper and fresh herbs in a little oil if you like them. It is good fat-side-up on the rack of an open pan (never a closed roaster, since that belies its name by steaming the meat), and basted frequently with pure fat until done. [I now use a patented V-shaped gadget, a kind of adjustable rack, for almost every kind of meat. And I almost never baste a roast anymore. Instead I roll it well in seasoned fat or olive oil, for an hour or so, and of course put it in the rack with the fattest side up.]

It is important that the basting liquid contain no water, nor indeed anything but good butter or beef-fat or oil, since anything else will open the seared pores and let the imprisoned juices flow away. Sheila Hibben, who writes with stern good sense about such matters, admits that in the case of a large roast a little water may be put under the rack, so that the bastings will not stick to the pan and be wasted.

Of course, the best gravy is one quite innocent of flour, in spite of what your grandmother would say. It is made by swirling a little boiling stock or water into the rich odorous pan as soon as the roast is removed. It is boiled for a scant five minutes, skimmed lightly, thickened with a little fresh butter, and strained into a hot sauceboat.

Long ago in Burgundy, when we ate the Sunday roast of beef or lamb, Madame Bonamour always put a big spoonful of this hot juice into the salad just before she stirred it. We liked it, especially if the bowl held escarole and what we rather indelicately called *pisse-en-lit*.

A rolled roast seems more economical at first sight, because you do not buy the rib bones. But you must remember that bones are conductors of heat and make meat cook about six minutes faster to the pound, thus cutting down on the fuel bill for the ribroast. Moreover, if you are going to splurge on anything as elegant as a roast, you might as well get the best, for nothing gives a better flavor to already fine meat than cooking it on the bones it grew on.

What used to be called the cheaper cuts of meat, such as the rump, can be cooked in a number of ways, but always following the main rules given in any good cookbook for pot-roasting or braising. One trouble with them is that they are seldom treated with due respect, but are seared in any kind of fat and then allowed to stew in some water until they are moderately tender, and more than a little stringy. They should be seasoned and watched with even greater care than a roast, since they have perhaps less dignity to start with.

Economically they are not very wise, since they take a long

time to cook, and demand attention. They can be delicious, of course (What meat-eater would not approve of Escoffier's Bœuf à la Mode?), but they are less adaptable than roast the second or third day, and thus become more of a luxury than what you may still like to call a necessity.

Probably the most popular kind of beef, after a ruddy roast, is broiled or grilled steak. This, to be at its best, should be what you yourself prefer: T-bone, porterhouse, tenderloin, and so on. You will undoubtedly have your own way of preparing it. You will, in your dreams at least . . . for such cuts of meat are far beyond the reach of wolf-dodgers.

You can buy a cheap cut, of course, like a round-bone steak, and have the butcher run it through a fantastic little electric machine called a Tender-Lux or some such thing. Then it comes out looking all nibbled, and supposedly tasting like the finest T-bone. [Now there are popular little flat pats of lean beef, frozen, which people keep assuring me are delicious "minute steaks." I have tried several times to agree . . . it would be so convenient if I could! . . . but I continue to find them stringy and innocuous and one more depressing proof of our gradual mediocrization, in the process of which we are forced to eat so many downright poor foods that we leap with sincere delight for the mediocre.]

Or you can make a mixture of equal parts of oil and vinegar, and rub it very hard into a tough steak, and then let it stand for two hours, with the fond conviction that the meat will be tenderer, which it probably will. [I use a mixture of oil and soy sauce now, on almost any cut of meat and many kinds of fish. This strange trick comes from a Japanese cook; he always coated fish with the sauce before putting it in the icebox, and it never smelled *fishy*. And it kept much longer and better, if need be. And best of all, it never tasted of soy sauce!]

Or you can save your meat money for quite a while, and buy

a good tenderloin and broil it as you and only you know how, and eat it like a man.

Of these courses the last is probably the most satisfying, esthetically if not dietetically, unless you are among those miserable ones who must have meat in some form every day because you always *have* had meat in some form every day. In that case, this little catalog of tricks on wolf-catching is not for you, and neither good sense nor the dictates of earthly war can still your carnivorous hunger.

Cheap is a word said in these times with a gallant laugh and a devil-may-care toss of the head, but it continues to modify the parts of a beef's body, like the chuck or the rump, which cannot possibly be sold at a higher price for broiling.

One way to use cheap meat is to buy that butt of gibes and snobbism, ground round steak. "Ground beef" is cheaper yet, but not a good investment because it contains so much fat and shrinks so in cooking that it is neither good for you nor economical.

The first thing to know about ground round steak is that it should not be that at all. Round steak is a fairly good cut of meat that can be bought in one piece and braised like a pot roast and prepared in various lengthy but delicious manners. It is foolish to grind it, since other parts of the meat can be ground into an even better-tasting mess for less money.

Butchers, usually, are very pleasant people, in spite of having at some time in their lives deliberately chosen to be butchers. They will assist your efforts to economize with amazing benevolence, and will agree with you that a piece of "lean end" or flank, stripped of its cartilage and fat and put once through the grinder, is as good meat as anybody could ask for.

Get the bones, if any, for your dog or your soup kettle, and the fat to chop later and fry crisp and dark brown for cabbage or even an omelet. Or make:

Crackling Bread

1 *cup cracklings, diced*	³⁄₄ *cup wheat flour*
1 *measure cornmeal pancake-*	½ *teaspoon soda*
flour	¼ *teaspoon salt*
or	1 *cup sour milk*
1½ *cups cornmeal*	

Cracklings are the pieces of meat remaining after the lard has been rendered from the fat (Pork in the South). Make the prepared batter or mix and sift together the dry ingredients, add the milk. Stir in the cracklings. Form into oblong cakes and place in a greased baking dish. Bake in hot oven (400°) about 30 minutes.

This is an old-fashioned recipe, except for the modern dodge of using a reputable prepared cornmeal mixture if you want to. It is a cheap and pleasant way to use something that otherwise would be wasted, and to give at least a savor of richness and solidity to a supper that might, without it, consist of plain cornpone and a glass of milk. [A delicious supper, cracklins or no.]

To return to your momentous purchase of some ground beef: with the meat in your hand, as it were, go home and unwrap it and cook it, or if you plan to keep it for a time in the icebox, be sure to bring it back to room-heat for a good two hours before using it. Then form it lightly into cakes, one for each person and rather on the large side if you are hungry, since one big one is much better than two or three little ones. [Unless you like meat very well done. I have trouble getting it any other way, unless I cook it myself.]

Heat a heavy skillet very hot, so that a drop of water dances and vanishes on its surface, which seems to look more stretched than you thought iron could look.

Put in the pats of beef. There will be a great smoke and smell, so windows should be open if possible. In about two minutes turn the cakes over with a spatula, and probably with your fingers masked in a pot-holder. There will be more smell. Keep the heat high for two more minutes or until the meat is thoroughly brown, and then slap on a tightly fitting lid and turn off whatever fuel you use. If you like your meat rare, you must act quickly from now on, but however you like it, the heat in the skillet will be sufficient. [It is more sensible to have the herbs ready before you start the pan-broiling of the meat. Now, especially for barbecues (this is fine for thick steaks, too), I put the herbs, wine, and a generous pat of butter in a bowl at least an hour before I'll want them, and then pour the mixture into the empty fuming skillet and, without covering it, let it blend for not more than a minute, just long enough to melt the butter, before I put it on the steak.]

Chop chives (or a little green onion split from end to end), parsley, basil, any other herbs you like and want, either fresh or dried . . . about two tablespoonfuls for each cake of beef. Have one-fourth of a cup red wine or tomato juice or vegetable stock for each one, and if the latter two are used add a little Worcestershire sauce. [Now and then very strong fresh coffee, one-fourth cup per serving, is delicious.]

Remove the cakes of meat to hot plates or a hot shallow casserole before they are quite done to your taste, since they will continue to cook. Then throw in the herbs and the liquid. There will be another great sizzle and fume. Put the cover on quickly, to catch all the first fine savor. In about fifty seconds, stir the mixture thoroughly to catch all the meat-essence in the pan, add a little butter, and put the mixture with a spoon over the cakes of meat. Serve at once, with hot French bread and a crisp green salad, and red wine or ale if you can and will.

Herb butter, a little blob on each cake just before serving, is perfect for this. [Here I obviously meant: "perfect for grilled beef cakes *instead* of the herb and wine sauce."] It is simply unsalted butter creamed with a little lemon juice and whatever finely chopped herbs you like. The mixture is packed into a jar, covered, and kept indefinitely in the icebox. If you are knowing about such things, you can have a different kind for every herb you know, and use them according to your hungers. [For instance, put 1 teaspoonful of basil butter in each small hollowed tomato, and grill for 5 minutes . . . delicious with lamb chops.]

They make almost any kind of meat or fish taste better than it meant to. They are not necessary, but they are *nice*, in the right sense of the word, so that eating meat becomes not a physical function, like breathing or defecating, but an agreeable and almost intellectual satisfaction of the senses.

II

Of course, there are many other ways to eat the flesh of animals than in its simplest states, raw or roasted or broiled or braised. According to some people, including the mournful ghosts of those masters who once ruled Paris kitchens and wrote letters to the *Times*, they are the only ways, since barbarians alone can stomach the sweet bloody savor of rare meat.

There are a thousand ways to cook it, all of them set forth in cookbooks of varied merit. The trouble with most of them is that they take too long and call for too many disguises that in themselves may seem inexpensive but added together make a surprising cost for the whole dish.

A stew, for instance: it is supposed to be the simplest of dishes, and probably in the far-gone days it was, when you threw a piece of meat and some water into a pot, and let them boil together until they had blended into one edible thing. Now, a stew means something richer, and can be a fine tantalizing dish indeed, full of braised meat and many vegetables and all bound together by a gravy heady with herbs and wine. We are proud to have raised it from its lowly place, and in so doing we have cheated ourselves of its first frugal goodness, for once having tasted the new kind, our palates are chilled by the starkness of the old.

Nonetheless, if you have the time and the fuel, make a stew for your soul's sake. It is a satisfying procedure, and can do no harm to man or beast. There is a different recipe for everyone who has ever thought of making one, but in general the rules are simple:

Braise the meat, which has been cut into small pieces, in fat. Season with whatever herbs you like [This means peppercorns, bay leaves, perhaps cloves stuck in an onion. The fresh herbs I would add only a few minutes before serving: basil or rosemary or marjoram, for instance, and parsley.], cover amply with stock or vegetable juice or water or wine, and simmer until almost done. Half-cook [. . . preferably braising first] any kinds of vegetables you like, except beets, which of course make a filthy color. Thicken the juice around the meat. Add the vegetables. Let the whole thing rest for a few hours . . . a day is better [. . . not better, *best*] and then bring to the boil and serve, preferably in soup-plates. The variations on this theme are as obvious as they are entertaining.

One good way to cook meat slowly without feeling completely extravagant is to arrange several other things that require the same temperature in the oven and can be cooked at the same time. A roast takes up most of the space in any modern oven I have ever seen, but there are other meats to bake in shallow pans or casseroles. A good one is:

Baked Ham Slice

1 *one-inch slice of ham (or thicker if you can afford it!)*	1 *sweet potato for each person* 1 *cup brown sugar*

1 *handful parsley*	1 *cup hot water [or cider, or*
2 *teaspoons hot mustard*	*white wine]*
1 *tart apple for each person*	

Pare the fat from the ham and mince with the chopped parsley and mustard. Spread thickly on the meat.

Slice the unpeeled apples ½ inch thick. Peel and slice the potatoes lengthwise ½ inch thick.

Place the ham in the center of a pan, with the apples and then the potatoes in a ring around it. Add the hot water, and sprinkle with the brown sugar.

Bake in a 325-350° oven, basting often, until the potatoes are tender. [This bakes faster if put in a shallow casserole and covered for the first half-hour.]

Another good way to cook ham, if you can afford it at all and want something that simmers along nicely with an ovenful of other things, is to get two slices and put them into a pan with chutney or any leftover preserves between the two, like a sandwich. Spread prepared mustard on the top, sprinkle some brown sugar over all, pour a little water or white wine or even stale beer into the dish, and cook for about an hour, basting frequently.

[Baked Ham in Cream is a richer dish, but very good indeed, now and then. There should be a generous, indeed a *Hungarian*, hand with the paprika, and the browning thickening cream in the flat dish should be spooned often over the slices of meat, gradually to form a pink-brown sauce, which sometimes curdles but with no danger to the whole.

This is a good thing to know about, with an air of luxury to it.

Baked Ham in Cream

*Have loaf-boiled ham cut in ½-inch slices. Cut each in two, place to-
gether like sandwiches. Place in baking pan with a little brown sugar
and plenty of paprika. Baste often with cream. Bake in moderate oven
for 25 minutes. Serve with pickled pears, figs, or prunes.]*

[Fine with casserole of noodles, butter, crumbs, and mushrooms sautéed.]

A flank steak is supposedly a cheap cut of meat, and the following recipe, while rather fussy to begin with, uses both the
meat and the moderate heat of an oven that we'll hope is well
filled with other things. There are of course many changes to be
rung on this:

Mock Duck

1 *flank steak, cut very thin*	*seasoning for dressing: sage,*
2 *cups bread crumbs*	*pepper, etc.*
1 *egg*	3 *tablespoons oil or fat*
	water or stock or wine

*Make a highly seasoned dressing according to your favorite rule. Mix
the egg into it.*

*Roll it into the steak, and tie tightly. Brown the roll in the hot fat, put
into a pan, and cover with whatever liquid you like: tomato juice, red
wine and water, vegetable stock . . . baste frequently. Cook until tender; the time will vary after one hour according to the thickness of the
roll. Remove the string before serving.*

This is good with fresh green beans or a plain salad, and brown
rice. The gravy can be thickened or not, as desired; personally,
I find that a little butter is enough change in it.

[One of the best things I can make, for a winter dinner, is the

Prune Roast whose recipe I give below. I am told by other cooks
that it is not wholly dependable: sometimes the prunes cook to
bits; sometimes the sauce is too thin or too thick. I have never
found this to be true, but I do know that no recipe in the world
is independent of the tides, the moon, the physical and emotional temperatures surrounding its performance. Having tak-
en all these into consideration, the only other questionables in
the problem are the meat and the prunes, and my one remark
about them is that they should be of good but not luxurious
quality. This roast, served on a generous platter and carved at
the table into thick slices, with ample sauce and a bowl of buttered noodles and a crisp bowl of salad greens, with good bread
and wine, and cheese to follow, makes a delicious dinner to
come upon. It is pungent and hearty, and the world seems more
real.

Prune Roast

4 to 5 pounds rump roast	½ cup cider vinegar
2 teaspoons salt	½ cup water
pepper	1 cup light brown sugar
2 cups washed, dried prunes	¼ teaspoon ground cloves
2 cups boiling water	1 teaspoon ground cinnamon

*Heat a heavy, deep pan on top of range. Add roast, turning so it will
brown on all sides. Sprinkle with salt and pepper. Add prunes and
water, cover, and simmer until tender (about 3 hours). Remove meat
from liquid to hot platter. Stir in vinegar, water, sugar, cloves, and cinnamon; cook rapidly until a thick sauce is formed. Pour sauce over and
around meat, serve immediately. Serves 8 to 10.*]

Almost all cookbooks, especially the endearing paperbound
volumes edited around the turn of this century by farflung Ladies' Guilds and other churchly societies, contain many such

recipes. They should be read with one canny eye on the cooking time, since fuel is an increasing expense and time itself is not a thing to be thrown about lightly.

Another point about which to be wary in the usually dependable recipes given in most such collections is the seasoning; it is, to put it mildly, a challenge to your inventive palate, since it either says, "Salt, pepper," or "Salt." Apparently any other condiments were considered foreign and perhaps even sacrilegious by members of the Saint James' Sewing Circle in 1902. Otherwise, recipes in such books are dependable, if you like such things.

III

One way to horrify at least eight out of ten Anglo-Saxons is to suggest their eating anything but the actual red fibrous meat of a beast. A heart or a kidney or even a sweetbread is anathema. It is too bad, since there are so many nutritious and entertaining ways to prepare the various livers and lights. They can become gastronomic pleasures instead of dogged voodoo, so that when you eat a stuffed baked bull's heart, or a grilled lamb's brain or a "mountain oyster," you need not choke them down with the nauseated resolve to be braver or wiser or more potent, but with plain delight. [I believe this more firmly than ever, but am years wearier in my fight. Now, when I want to eat what English butchers call "offal," I wait until everyone has gone to the Mid-South Peoria Muezzins' Jamboree and Ham-bake, and then make myself a dainty dish.]

I must admit that my own first introduction to *tête de veau* was a difficult one for a naive American girl. The main trouble, perhaps, was that it was not a veal's head at all, but half a veal's head. There was the half-tongue, lolling stiffly from the neat half-mouth. There was the one eye, closed in a savory wink. There was the lone ear, lopped loose and faintly pink over the odd wrinkles of the demi-forehead. And there, by the single pallid nostril, were three stiff white hairs.

At first I thought the world was too much with me, and wondered how gracefully I could leave it. Then what I am sure was my good angel made me stay, and eat, and finally ask for more, for *tête de veau*, when it is intelligently prepared, can be a fine exciting dish.

["I don't go much out," as a German-American friend of mine says, but even so I have lived about three-fourths of my life in the United States and I have *never* been served anything even faintly suggestive of the undisguisable anatomy of a boiled calf's head, in this my homeland. The nearest I have ever come to it was, when I was little, delicious cold shaky slices of Head Cheese for summer lunch, and even that was genteelly called "cold shape" by my English aunt who had the courage to make it for Southern Californians . . . until I grew up enough to make it myself. I give her basic recipe, to be flavored to differing tastes, and then my own version of the classic rules of Tête de Veau: Escoffier, for instance, dictates using a "white court-bouillon," but I like a less subtly delicate broth to cook the meat in . . . I like it cooked in halves, *à l'anglaise*, but served with a vinaigrette sauce instead of the proper "boat of parsley sauce" . . . and so on.

Aunt Gwen's Cold Shape (!)

1 calf head, quartered
  salt, pepper, bay, herbs as
    desired
	½ cup lemon juice
	  or
	1 cup dry white wine

Remove most of fat, and the brains (save for another dish), ears, eyes, and snout (a kindly butcher will do this for the finicky). Soak for ½ hour in cold water, wash off, cover with cold water, and simmer until the meat starts to fall from the bones. Drain in large colander over another kettle, saving all the cooking liquor. Dice the meat ("in pretty pieces," Aunt

Gwen directed), add the stock amply to cover, and mix gently with sea-
soning to taste. Simmer for 3/4 hour, add the lemon juice or wine, and
pour into a mold. Cover with a cloth, weight well, and chill. Serve in
slices. (Aunt Gwen used bread-pans for the molds, clean bricks for the
weights . . . and there were always cucumber-chips on the platter.)

Tête de Veau

1	*calf head*	1	*small head celery or 3 large*
2	*or 3 quarts water*		*stalks*
1	*carrot*	1	*lemon in quarters*
1	*onion*		*salt, pepper, 2 bay leaves, 6*
			cloves

Have head cut in half. Soak for 1 hour in cold water. Boil water and rest
of ingredients for 10 minutes. Drain halves, add to liquid, and simmer,
well covered, for about 1½ hours or until the cheeks are tender. (The
tongue and brain can be removed, the former to be cooked with the head,
the latter added to the bouillon for the final ¼ hour of simmering. They
should be nicely trimmed, sliced, and served with the halves.) Drain,
and serve at once surrounded by parsley, with a sauceboat of vinaigrette
made of 1 part vinegar, 1 part of the cooking liquor, and 2 parts oil, with
the required seasonings. Or . . . drain, rub carefully with a cloth soaked
in lemon juice to keep the flesh from darkening, and chill well. Serve
surrounded by small green onions, capers, parsley, and sliced cucum-
bers, with a sauceboat of vinaigrette to taste.]

Why is it worse, in the end, to see an animal's head cooked and
prepared for our pleasure than a thigh or a tail or a rib? If we are
going to live on other inhabitants of this world we must not
bind ourselves with illogical prejudices, but savor to the fullest
the beasts we have killed.

People who feel that a lamb's cheek is gross and vulgar when
a chop is not are like the medieval philosophers who argued
about such hairsplitting problems as how many angels could

dance on the point of a pin. If you have these prejudices, ask yourself if they are not built on what you may have been taught when you were young and unthinking, and then if you can, teach yourself to enjoy some of the parts of an animal that are not commonly prepared.

Sweetbreads of course are in somewhat snobbish repute, and are indeed worthy of their reputation. Unfortunately they are expensive.

The same is true of liver, which is supposed to be one of the best things in the world to eat if you are anemic. It should be beef or calf liver, since pork liver is fat and heavy to the taste, and according to some authorities actively impure.

There are many fine recipes for preparing liver, but it should always be cooked swiftly so as not to be toughened. It is good the next day, cooked with other leftovers with some sherry added to the sauce, and brown rice to eat with it. (It is also delicious cold, with a glass of beer and some fresh-ground pepper, and a few sprigs of parsley, if you're of the same turn of mind as I am.)

Tongue is of course more acceptable socially than some of the other functional parts of a beast's anatomy. Its main trouble as an economical thing to prepare is that it takes a long time to cook. It is a deceptively mild meat, and needs some characterful sauce well laced with condiments or wine to stand by it.

Brains are, to my mind, unfortunately coupled with scrambled eggs on most menus. The combination is an unpleasant one, because of the similar textures of the two things. Instead, I think brains should be cooked so that they are crisp, and should be served with crisp things, to offset the custard-like quality of their interiors. The following recipe from Barcelona is a good example, and is delicious with fresh peas, hot toast, and fruit:

Calves' Brains

1 *pair calves' brains*	*parsley, 5 or 6 sprigs*
¼ *cup good vinegar, or 1 lemon*	*salt and pepper*
3 *tablespoons butter or good oil*	

Blanch brains in boiling water. Remove outer skin, taking care not to break inner tissue. Place in cold water for 1 hour. Drain, sprinkle with vinegar or lemon juice, and let stand ½ hour.

Drain and salt the brains and fry until golden brown in the hot fat. Place on a hot serving plate and fry the parsley. Add the remaining vinegar or lemon juice to the pan, heat well, and pour over the brains. Garnish with the crisp parsley, and freshly ground pepper. [If you like deep-frying, there are fine tricks to play with various crisp "fritters" made of brains or sweetbreads.]

Another vital part of a beef is the heart, which is not well enough known as a meat unusually rich in vitamins and minerals too. A large heart should be stuffed with a regular poultry-dressing, aromatic with fresh or dried herbs, and basted often with fat of rich stock in a slow oven until it is tender. The process is rather long, but is well worth it if you can fit other things into the oven at the same time.

Smaller hearts can be split, braised, and simmered in the oven or a heavy skillet with strips of bacon, until they are tender. Then put them under the broiler long enough to brown.

Small veal or lamb hearts can be sliced thin, braised quickly in hot fat, and then simmered in stock with cubed vegetables and herbs for a fine savory stew to eat with rice. A little sherry and sour cream stirred in just before serving make the flavors even more satisfying.

Another way to use a large heart, which will take much less time than would baking it whole, is to grind it. Mix it with a ground onion, celery if you like it, a couple of eggs, whatever stock or tomato juice you have in the icebox, and some bread crumbs if it seems too moist. Season it with fresh pepper, a little dill, some sweet marjoram . . . any herbs you like. Pack it into a bread-pan or make it into a loaf, and bake it an hour or until done in a moderate oven, basting frequently. [I would now say: "*At least* two hours." Long slow cooking makes it especially good and firm, for slicing for a cold buffet or for sandwiches.]

Kidneys are in better repute than some of the other innards, mainly because English arbiters of our gastronomic likes and dislikes eat them broiled, and right they are. There is nothing much better than a sizzling skewerful of little lamb kidneys, bacon, mushrooms, and maybe a few dwarf-size tomatoes, all dipped in butter and twilled for five minutes or so in a hot broiler: nothing much better, that is, if you like it. Some people do not. They *loathe* kidneys, with a loathing that is impregnable to temptation. There is nothing to do about it, apparently, but remember not to serve them to those unfortunate souls.

One good basic recipe, which can be varied indefinitely and is good warmed over or made in a chafing dish or on an outdoor barbecue, is:

Kidneys in Sherry

2 *tablespoons butter or good oil*	½ *cup sherry*
1 *sweet onion, minced*	*watercress*
1 *pair veal kidneys*	*toast, rice, or whatever*
seasoning	

Wash kidneys and cut into little pieces. Brown the onion in the fat and add the meat. Add seasoning (salt, pepper, fresh-chopped parsley or basil or whatever herb you like). Add the sherry and simmer five minutes. Serve very hot, with the watercress as a garnish.

This recipe I got from Spain, but it is the same everywhere. Different herbs are used, or lemon juice instead of sherry, or sour cream [one cup thick sour cream, just after the sherry: very good with kasha or wild rice, very Smetanaish] is put in at the last, or a little brandy is poured in. Mushrooms are browned with the onion in the fat. Capers and shaved almonds are tossed in just before serving; the mixture is put into hollowed tomatoes and grilled.

In other words, you can do what you like, remembering always that kidneys have a strong pungent taste that needs to be curbed by the even stronger flavors of herbs and liquors.

A very quick dish that is inexpensive, and good with a salad and cheese and coffee for supper, is:

Sausage Pie (or Sardine Pie)

½ pound sausage [or bacon] (or ½ can sardines) tomato sauce biscuit-mix	1 teaspoon grated onion or chopped green onion

Spread sausage [or bacon or fish] thin in pie-pan or shallow casserole. Let heat in quick oven and pour off almost all fat. (Leave oil on sardines.)

Make one-half usual baking powder biscuit, mixing with tomato sauce [. . . or meat stock. It is a question of flavors. One good combination with bacon strips is milk in the biscuit-mix, plus a generous half-cup of grated cheese.] instead of milk or water. Add the onion and any chopped herbs you like. Pour over the sausage, and bake in hot oven until firm and brown [. . . about 20 minutes].

Shrimps are good in this pie too; indeed, it came from Portugal, where they used to grow on bushes, practically.

Leftover meats are always fun to cope with, and one of the nicest ways, which for some reason always surprises people, is in canelloni. Canelloni are simply small unsweetened pancakes like delicate *enchiladas*, which are filled with what the recipe discreetly calls "any plausible mixture": meat, fish, herbs, eggyolks, on and on.

They are rolled and laid in a shallow dish, on spinach puree if you like. Then they are sprinkled with grated cheese and browned quickly. [A nice thing about them is that the pancakes can be made several hours in advance (they should be thin, like French *crêpes*). So can the "mixture." They should be combined at the last. If something in a sauce is used for the filling, like creamed chicken, some of the sauce should be put over the whole.]

There are always curries, of course, which are really not curries at all, but simply leftover meat served in a gravy flavored with curry powder. [This is a horrible definition, and only the next sentence saves me from gastronomical guilt.] They can be very good or ghastly, according to the cook. The following recipe is uninspired, but dependable.

An English Curry

1 onion, sliced	¼ cup vinegar
3 to 4 tablespoons fat or 2 slices bacon	¼ cup water
	1 cup tomato sauce
1½ tablespoons hot curry powder	leftover meat and gravy

Fry onion golden brown in fat or with chopped bacon. Mix the curry, water, and vinegar, and add to the onion. [Mix briskly over hot flame; this develops the curry powder's flavor.] Add the tomato sauce, and cook 5 minutes. Cut the meat into small pieces, add it to the sauce with any of its gravy, and cook until heated through. This is better for standing a few hours [Not much better. A real curry is, but this hasty makeshift must sink or swim, to quote myself a bit further down, on the basic goodness of its immediate contents.], and should be served with rice and a syrupy preserve (figs, peaches).

Another good way to use meat, aside from the time-honored and never to be scorned Third-Day Hash, which like curry sinks or swims with the cook who compounds it, is this:

Turkish Hash

2 *tablespoons butter or fat*	1 *cup tomatoes, cooked or fresh*
1 *chopped onion*	1 *tablespoon horseradish*
½ *cup uncooked brown rice*	*(optional)*
1 *cup water or stock*	*salt, pepper, any desired*
1½ *cups cooked diced meat*	*herbs*
1 *bud garlic*	

Cook the butter, onion, and rice in a heavy skillet until brown, turning often. Add the rest of the ingredients, mix thoroughly, and cover the skillet tightly. As soon as it steams, turn the fire very low, and cook for about 20 minutes or until done.

Lin Yutang, more than once, has written that it is a shock to him to see how much an average American family spends on meat. He says that we could cut our bills in half, and that is quite a lot, by cooking as the Chinese people do and using more vegetables.

It is all a question, according to him, of marrying the tastes of the meat and the green things in the kitchen, instead of letting them meet each other for the first time "when served on the table in their respective confirmed bachelorhood and unspoiled virginity."

In spite of inventions and conceits, however, and the dogged appliance of good common sense, meat continues to be the most expensive part of the modern diet.

Each person must evolve his own system of eating as much as possible of what he wants and needs. For myself, if I were rationed to two ounces of meat a day, as many of our brothers are (to mention only the more fortunate ones) [true today, only more so] I should prefer to save it for a week perhaps, and make a nice stew of it, or fix it in some way so that for one meal at least I would feel myself safe and fat again in the time of plenty.

Other people would not agree with me. But for all of us, no matter what our tastes, life would be simpler and the wolf would howl less loudly if we could adjust our minds to admit, even if we never quite believed it, that a tender sizzling rare grilled tenderloin was a luxury instead of a necessity.

How to Make a Pigeon Cry

Here's a pigeon so finely roasted, it cries, Come, eat me!
Polite Conversation, JONATHAN SWIFT

For centuries men have eaten the flesh of other creatures not only to nourish their own bodies but to give more strength to their weary spirits. A bull's heart, for example, might well bring bravery; oysters, it has been whispered, shed a new potency not only in the brain but in certain other less intellectual regions. And pigeons, those gentle flitting creatures, with the soft voices and their miraculous wings in flight, have always meant peace, and refreshment to sad humans.

Perhaps it is an old wives' tale; perhaps it is a part of our appetites more easily explained by *The Golden Bough* than by a cook or doctor: whatever the reason, a roasted pigeon is and long has been the most heartening dish to set before a man bowed down with grief or loneliness. In the same way it can reassure a timid lover, or comfort a woman weak from childbirth.

It is not easy to find pigeons, these days. Most of the ones you know about in the city are working for the government. In the country there are few farmers, anymore, that have kept their dovecotes clean and populous . . . and fewer hired men who will kill the pretty birds properly by smothering them. By far the easiest way to make a pigeon cry, "Come, eat me!" is to buy it, all cleaned and trussed, from a merchant.

It is usually expensive, in a mild way. [How can extravagance be mild? And what is mild about a minimal $1.25 per bird? But I still say it is worth it, now and then.] But if you like the idea at all, it is worth saving your meat-money for a few days, and making a party of it; eating a roasted pigeon is one of the few things that can be done all by yourself and in sordid surroundings with complete impunity and a positive reaction of well-being. [And for two, four, or six people who know each other well enough to eat with their fingers, there is no pleasanter supper than hot or cold roasted pigeons, with kasha or wild rice and undressed watercress and good bread . . . and, of course, plenty of good red wine.]

[It seems impossible that there is, apparently, no recipe for kasha in this book so trustingly dedicated to my fellow philosophers in Operation Wolf. Kasha is a fine thing. In spite of unhappy political as well as gastronomical overtones just now, I must say that Russians are strong people because of it (. . . and cabbage and black bread and sour cream and floods of hothot-*hot* tea). It can be bought most easily, at least in Western America, from "health food stores." Package directions should be followed carefully, for unfortunately some of the stuff is precooked now, and turns into a horrid mush if you go on with the old routine of slow steaming. Properly prepared, kasha makes a wonderful aromatic nutty accompaniment to meat or fowl, and alone it is delicious, with an extra pat of butter, and combined with mushrooms it is heavenly, and and and. . . .

Kasha

2 *cups kasha (whole or cracked groats)*	*butter or fat, about ³⁄₅ tablespoon*

1 or 2 fresh eggs   salt, pepper
4 or more cups hot water or
    stock

Put kasha into heavy skillet and mix egg into it until each grain is coated. Stir often over very low fire, until the grains are glazed and nut-like. Add liquid slowly, put fat in center, and cover closely, to cook until fluffy and tender (about ¾ hour). Season and add more butter if wished. Serve.]

I have eaten a great many pigeons here and there, and I know that the best was one I cooked in a cheap Dutch oven on a one-burner gas-plate in a miserable lodging. The wolf was at the door, and no mistake; until I filled the room with the smell of hot butter and red wine, his pungent breath seeped through the keyhole in an almost visible cloud.

Supper took about half an hour to prepare (I could have done it more quickly, but there was no reason for it), and long before I was ready to put the little brown fuming bird on my one Quimper plate, and pour out my second glass of wine, I heard a sad sigh and then the diminishing click of his claws as he retreated down the hall and out into the foggy night. I had routed him, because of the impertinent recklessness of roasting a little pigeon and savoring it intelligently and voluptuously too.

This is the way I cooked that innocent brown bird, and the way, with small variations, I have often treated other ones since then:

Roast Pigeon

1 *pigeon*   *red wine (or cider, beer,*
1 *lemon*   *orange juice, tomato juice,*
2 *slices fat bacon (or 2*   *stock . . .), about a cupful*
    tablespoons butter or oil)   *water*
    parsley   *salt, pepper*

Melt the fat. [If bacon is used, cook it until crisp, and then remove it until time to serve it alongside, over, or even under the little bird.] See that the bird is well plucked, and rub her thoroughly with a cut lemon and the seasoning. Push the parsley into the belly. Braise well in the hot fat.

Add the liquid, put on the lid quickly, and cook slowly for about 20 minutes, basting two or three times. If you are going to eat the bird cold, put into a covered dish so that it will not dry out. [And if hot, make a pretty slice of toast for each bird, butter it well (or spread it with a bit of good pâté de foies for Party!), and place the bird upon it. Swirl about one cup of dry good wine and 2 tablespoonfuls butter in the pan, for 4 birds, and spoon this over each one immediately, and serve.]

The accompaniments to this little bird (I ate it hot) were what was left of the red wine, which was a Moulin à Vent at twenty-six cents a quart, a rather dry piece of bread, which was perfect for sopping all the juice from the plate, and three long satiny heads of Belgian endive. Celery hearts would have been just as good, I think, or *almost* as good.

Another heartening thing to eat, made from a wild creature, has always been associated with good-fellowship and even a bit of jolly poaching, if not with the reconciliation of man and his fate. Rabbit, or hare, or *lièvre*; it makes a strong and yet delicate dish no matter how it is prepared, if you remember one or two subtle tricks to play upon it first.

Always soak the hare for an hour or so in salty water, which has lemon juice or about a quarter-cup of vinegar in it. Then dry it well before cooking. A small piece of fat pork, either salted or fresh, will make the flavor of the meat much richer if they are cooked together. A tender hare [or domestic rabbit, for that matter] can well be prepared for frying like a chicken, but it is a dry meat and is usually better with a sauce around it. Almost all such recipes begin with soaking and then braising the meat, and letting it simmer slowly in a juice that can be as your wishes dictate. The following has always pleased me:

Rabbit in Casserole

1	large or 2 smaller rabbits		salt, pepper, speck of clove,
	hot water		etc.
	salt	1	cup stock or water
	lemon juice (or vinegar)	1	cup red wine
3	slices fat bacon	1	handful chopped fresh herbs
4	tablespoons butter		(parsley, sage, etc.)
4	tablespoons olive or other oil	1	cup tomato juice
½	cup flour		

Cut up rabbit and soak for an hour or more in the hot salty water and lemon juice. Cut the bacon into small pieces and fry in the butter and oil.

Dry the meat, and shake well in a paper bag with the flour and condiments. Fry in the hot fat, turning often until each piece is very brown.

Add the stock, wine, and herbs, and cover closely. Cook slowly about one hour or until tender.

Remove the meat to a hot casserole. Add the tomato juice to the skillet and stir thoroughly until the sauce is thick and bubbling. Pour over the rabbit and serve.

This recipe can of course be varied according to what supplies you have and how much time and money you want to spend on its preparation. Another good one that takes longer and is worth it, is a kind of composite of *civet de lièvre*, hasenpfeffer, and

Jugged Hare

1	large or 2 small rabbits		butter
	water		oil
	vinegar or wine	1	cup sour cream
1	onion, sliced		
	salt, pepper, cloves, bay		
	leaves		

Cut up the rabbit and lay in a jar. Cover with equal parts of water and

either vinegar or wine; add the onion and spices. Allow this to soak two days, turning the meat at least once.

Remove the meat, and brown thoroughly in a mixture of oil and butter, turning it often. When it is well browned, cover gradually with the pickling sauce, as much as you want. Let it simmer for about half an hour, or until tender. Before serving stir the sour cream into it.

This dish, like any other honorable stew, is best served with noodles or rice or French bread to help with its dark-brown delectable juices, and a salad of green leaves from the garden. [Classic accompaniments are Brussels sprouts, pureed chestnuts, watercress, fried bread spread with tart jelly, variations of *sauce espagnole*, sliced lemons, fried hominy, fresh dill somewhere or other, dumplings, stewed prunes or pears, grilled mushrooms . . . !] If red wine is a part of it, the same honest, rather crude wine is meant to drink along with it (since, *bien entendu*, you would not use a wine anywhere in cooking that was disagreeable to drink by itself). If the sauce has been helped by plain stock, a rather heavy ale is good, since it relates itself well to the rich aromatic flavors of the dish.

It may seem that such birds as partridges are far from the cupboards of good wolf-cookers, but now and then a friend sends you one, or there is a little stock of them at the market begging to be bought.

The following recipe, given to me by a Nivernais farm woman who to her own constant surprise was a famous lecturer on Greek at a French university, can be used for any poultry or small game that may seem dry or a little tough, although it is meant for partridge or pheasant. I have cooked an ancient chicken and an equally experienced rabbit according to its formula.

Partridge or Pheasant
with Sauerkraut

salt and pepper	1½ *pounds sauerkraut*
2 *small or 1 large bird (or 1 rabbit)*	1 *cup peeled and sliced apples*
bacon slices	1 *cup dry white wine (or half and half with water or*
3 *tablespoons butter or good oil*	*vegetable stock)*
	1 *tablespoon flour*

Rub birds with cut lemon, and salt and pepper them. Wrap with the bacon and tie securely with twine. Heat the fat and brown the birds.

Wash the drained sauerkraut (unless it is very mild, then just drain it). Place a layer of it with the apple slices in the bottom of a casserole and imbed the birds. Cover with the rest of the kraut and apple, add the liquid, and cover closely. Let simmer very slowly for about 2 hours.

Put the birds on a hot plate, and thicken the kraut with the flour. Make nests in it, and replace the birds in them, ready to serve.

[An even better dish, I feel since I have become the willing victim of an annual donation of frozen pheasant, is the recipe I give herewith. I am sorry to say that I have never handled freshly killed game in this country, but I have coped, for want of a better procedure, with an infinitude of withered, almost sexless, apparently ageless birds in their repulsive peaky feathers and their gaseous envelopes filled with invisible but still potent "dry ice." I have done horrendous things with them, and then admitted my own courage and downed my own successes. (Once I roasted ducks and pheasants in the same big pan . . . it was a marvellous thing, which I have never before confessed to.) This present recipe is an excellent rule for enjoying a bird of questionable dates (birth, death, all that), and as far as I know it would be somewhat better with one of *proper* timing.

Normandy Pheasant

Brown pheasant in butter. Quarter, peel, mince, and slightly toss in hot butter 6 medium-sized apples and 3 small minced onions. Place pheasant on mixture in terrine, sprinkle with about ½ cup fresh cream, cover, and cook in moderate oven about ½ hour.]

Most of the ways for cooking poultry and game with economy seem to end inevitably as one form or another of the primeval stew. There are several reasons, most of which are followed almost intuitively by people who want to eat the best possible food for the least amount of money and time.

Roasting, for instance, except in the case of very small birds like pigeons, takes two hours or so of almost constant attention with a basting spoon, whereas a stew, after the meat is first braised, can be left to its own devices for about the same length of time. (You should make sure that the fire is under control and the casserole reasonably filled with liquid before you leave it.)

A roasted bird or little beast, while one of the most delicious things to eat that man has invented, emerges from the oven with no accompaniment except its own few unconsumed essences, and more often than not it has shrunk some into the bargain. A stew, on the other hand, seems to make a much bigger meal, because other things are usually cooked with it and have absorbed some of its flavor, and at the same time it is making a generous amount of fine odorous sauce that can be eaten with the meat and also with rice or potatoes or the humble and almighty crust of bread.

As for frying poultry, who could deny the delights of young pullets put to this test, if they are properly treated? Indeed, to believe the menus everywhere in America, fried chicken is neck and neck with grilled steak as the dish most people will order when they "eat out."

On the other hand (the wolf's side of the question!), it is an expensive job to fry enough young chicken in good fat for a family, and accompany it with the rich gravy, the mashed potatoes, the buttered peas, the hot biscuits and honey, and finally the pie or ice cream, that since our country first stood on its own legs have meant Company or Sunday Dinner.

A frying chicken, if he escapes being broiled, should weigh about three pounds. If he keeps on growing and in turn escapes being roasted at about five pounds, he is ready (albeit unwilling) "to grace the fricassée pot with aplomb and elegance," Mrs. Mazza says, "still young, still tender, but mature and at his zenith of plumpness." And when you consider the various exciting sauces that can smother his neat sections, once he is browned in honest fat, you wonder at ever believing that the only good way to prepare him was fried in a skillet.

One thing to remember about cooking any fowl, whether wild or domesticated, is that a good scrub with a cut lemon, never water, will make it tenderer and will seal in its flavors. Another thing is that a mixture of butter and oil or fat is the best one for braising it: it seems to make an evener and more delicious brown.

If you have bought or been given a chicken (it is very nice indeed, these days, to have generous friends who live in the country and send you unexpected lagniappes!), cut it up, scrub it with lemon, and season it. Try a little cinnamon and allspice with the omnipresent salt and pepper. After it is brown, put in a generous handful of chopped herbs (parsley, rosemary, basil, thyme, whatever you and your whims can pluck or purchase), and a minced clove of garlic. Add a cup or so of tomato, either fresh or canned, and some dry white wine. Stir the whole thing, cover and let simmer until tender.

In Italy such a savory dish used to be called *pollo in umido*. [One Yankee standby I have never been able to savor with more than a clinical interest is stewed hen with dumplings and gravy. I have probably eaten it at its best, and I am sure I have eaten it at its worst, and I still find it a pale thing.] It varied a little in every district or village—in every kitchen, really—but always it was served with the sauce in a separate dish, to be eaten with the spaghetti or the polenta.

You can see, probably, how good it would be. It is one of those "naturals" that take their own dignified place in any meal, whether it is served in midsummer on a breathless balcony, or in the windy months beside a fire. Whatever its milieu, it is eminently satisfying, and at the same time a great deal easier on your pocketbook than the same amount of chicken Maryland, even though you add wine and mushrooms and perhaps a crazy dash of pickled capers or nasturtium seeds.

You can eat it tomorrow, too . . . and fool the wolf . . . and if it is necessary, comfort yourself by reading this strange quotation from Wesker's *Secrets of Nature*, which was published in 1660:

Take the goose, pull off the feathers, make a fire about her, not too close for smoke to choke her, or burn her too soon, not too far off so she may escape. Put small cups of water with salt and honey . . . also dishes of apple sauce. Baste goose with butter. She will drink water to relieve thirst, eat apples to cleanse and empty her of dung. Keep her head and heart wet with a sponge. When she gets giddy from running and begins to stumble, she is roasted enough. Take her up, set her before the guests: she will cry as you cut off any part and will be almost eaten before she is dead. . . . It is mighty pleasant to behold.

How to Pray for Peace

Pray for peace and grace and spiritual food,
For wisdom and guidance, for all these are good,
But don't forget the potatoes.
                              Prayer and Potatoes, J. T. PETTEE

It is easy to think of potatoes, and fortunately for men who have not much money it is easy to think of them with a certain safety. Potatoes are one of the last things to disappear, in times of war, which is probably why they should not be forgotten in times of peace.

They can be bought, until things change even more radically than the pessimists predict, in sacks at almost any market. There are various names for them, and nice ones too: Idaho Russet, White Rose, Late Beauty of Hebron. They are a vegetable, white inside and shirted in a fine silky brown coat that is like a thin layer of cork, but much more delicious when washed and cooked with the rest.

Potatoes, like most other vegetables and animals, soon die when their skins are removed, so that it is better to boil or bake them entire, and then remove the delicate coat if you prefer to eat them peeled.

If your taste buds are truly civilized, however, one of the best meals in the world is a pot of medium-sized unpeeled potatoes, boiled briskly in hot water until they are done, and then drained and "shook" over the flame for a minute until the brown coverings split. Either throw in a handful of chopped fresh herbs like parsley and marjoram and chives (or green onion), and some butter, and shake it all around [A celestial variation is to add to fresh green peas, cooked rapidly in a little chicken broth or water and then drained and tossed generously in sweet butter, half their amount of small new potatoes, cooked and of course unpeeled, and half *their* amount of little braised white onions.] or pour the vegetables straightway into a hot bowl and eat them the way the Swiss do, with a good nubbin of cheese and a good gout of sweet butter and coarse salt and pepper for each biteful. This, with a glass of milk or some white wine and fruit, is a fit supper for Lucullus.

If your oven is going at about 300 to 350°, wash a few even-sized potatoes, dry them, and rub them with a little oil or butter. You can split them if you are in a hurry, buttering their cut sides, of course. As soon as they are tender [. . . or better yet, I now know, when you first put them in the oven] pierce them with a fork to keep them from growing soggy, and then eat them, if you are hungry, with plenty of butter and salt and fresh-ground pepper, not forgetting the delicate nutlike brown skin.

Or hollow them gently, stir the white part briskly with an egg and some seasonings, and put it back in the shells, with a little cheese or a couple of baby sausages on top to brown under the broiler. (These last potatoes can be made several hours before they are to be broiled, and are especially good in winter.)

[It is too bad that so many people have either not yet acquired a healthy acquaintanceship with good potato soup, or have had it shocked out of them by early exposure to a pasty and unreasonable facsimile. Most people I know fall into one of these categories, until I give them, for a winter lunch or a Sunday-night supper or some such loose-jointed feast, a steaming tureen of soup based, just as loose-jointedly, on the following rule:

Quick Potato Soup
(Referred to sardonically by my father as Poor Man's Potage . . .)

¼ *pound good butter*	2 *quarts whole milk*
4 *large potatoes*	*salt, pepper, minced parsley*
4 *large onions*	*if agreeable*

Melt the butter in large kettle, or in fireproof casserole in which the soup can be served. Grate the clean potatoes into it. (I like to leave them un-peeled, but the soup is not so pretty unless chopped fresh herbs, added at the last, change its natural whiteness enough to hide the bits of brown skin . . .) Grate the peeled onions into it . . . or slice them very thin. Heat the mixture to bubble-point, stirring well. Then reduce the heat, and cover closely for about 10 minutes or until the vegetables are tender but not mushy, shaking the pot now and then to prevent sticking. Add more butter (or chicken-fat) if it seems wise. Heat the milk to the boiling point but not beyond, add slowly to the pot, season, and serve. Varia-tions of this recipe are obvious. One of my father's favorites is the last-minute addition of a cup or so of cooked minced clams. A half-pound of grated fresh mushrooms, added to the vegetables just before pouring in the hot milk, is fine. And so on and so on.]

These are such simple procedures, and other ways of cooking starchy foods are so simple too, that it is almost shocking how badly they are usually done. Rice, for instance, which is one of the most primitive foods in the world, if you consider the num-ber of uneducated people who eat it: more often than not it is stodgy, sticky, and unappetizing, or else rinsed until it is as tasteless as library paste, and probably less nourishing.

There are two ways to boil rice correctly. [How arbitrary can you be? I should have said: "*I think* there are . . .!" I still think so, but am open to persuasion now, being older and hopefully wiser.] One way is to pour one well-rinsed cup of it slowly into a lot of rapidly boiling salted water (at least three quarts), and let it race around until a grain of it smashes between the fingers.

If it boils quickly it will never stick. A small dab of butter [or even better, a dollop of good oil . . .] will keep the pot from boiling over, and not harm the flavor. When the rice is almost done, it should be drained into a colander (the water should be saved if your family eats a lot of soups), and then rinsed thoroughly with cold water. Then it should be heated again by a quick immersion in boiling water before serving, or it can be steamed to the proper temperature. [I still prefer the steaming, but if I could I would rewrite this whole procedure. I suggest that anyone who acknowledges the value of good cookery in a life deliberately full of love, happiness, and health (that is, anyone who *cares* about human dignity!) read several other books and from them and this one and most of all from *himself* produce his own decision.]

The other accepted method is sometimes called Chinese and sometimes Indian, but it is a good one if you can do it. I think the secret is to have a thick pot, with a good lid, and a stove that will turn almost completely off without blowing out.

Chinese Rice

1 *cup rice*	1½ *cups water*

Wash rice thoroughly in several changes of water, until there is no cloudiness. Put the rice in a pot, add the water, and bring to a boil. Boil 5 minutes with the lid off. Turn the flame lower and let the water boil away. Then turn the flame to its lowest point, put on the lid, and heat 20 minutes without stirring. A crust should form at the bottom, but it should not burn.

The last sentence in this recipe is a warning, but do not let it disturb you if you like rice and want to eat it when it is at its best; I have never yet cooked it this way without having it stick to the pot, but by dint of great care I have never burned it. And each time I've done it it has seemed simpler. [If the crust has not changed color, I put some stock or milk on it and make anything from a soup to a pudding from the fine soft grains that gradually detach themselves into the liquid . . . certainly a most pleasant way to clean the pot!]

Rice, whether cooked this way or that, is an ideal accompaniment to almost any dish that has a savorous sauce with it. It is a godsend for making leftovers into gastronomical adventures, and can stand to be left in the icebox and then reheated more than once. As a dessert it can be used with eggs and milk and raisins, as what child of the fin de siècle does not know? Or it is good, if your tastes are simple, cold with a little brown sugar and milk, for supper or an icebox snack . . . a quick return to the nursery, which can be soothing indeed.

Brown rice is better for you than polished rice; it has more of the rich nutritive coat left on it. It takes a little longer to cook than other kinds. White rice, especially if you can still find the short chubby Chinese variety, has a lightness about it and is dry and fluffy when it is correctly prepared. [A new "instant-cook" rice is everywhere. I use rice so simply that it must be very good, but cooks who make myriad rings–molds–doodads tell me this is perfection. I continue to remember the water I once poured off a pound of it, after a few minutes of washing: it was turgid with added chemicals.]

Another way to cook rice, which seems more intelligent than boiling it when you think of the dread pasty monotony of most rice as it is served in our country, is to cook it in oil and then with other things, instead of in plain water. It can be called a *risotto*, or a *sopa de arroz*, or a *pilaf*, but what it is is rice browned gently in oil or butter, with any herbs you like, and then cooked without stirring in a heavy pan with wine or stock until it is tender. Meat can be added, or mushrooms, and saffron in the old days in Milano, or pepper sausage, and almonds and raisins in Singapore, before the causeway was blown up.

It is important [not *too* important, I have decided with the inevitable and perhaps cynical laissez-faire of Time], with any of these *risotti*, to rub the rice clean in a towel first, and then not to stir things after the liquid has been added. Always have more juice than you think you will need, and add it a cup at a time as it disappears, so that at the end the mixture is dry and fluffy, without visible sauce.

Almost any quick mixtures that are made with a modicum of gastronomic intelligence and a generous hand with the sauce are good served with rice, which can be leftover and reheated, or even taken from a can. [Cooked rice from a can? Was I dreaming? Should I ask my grocer? Where have I *been*?! Mea culpa.] Noodles and spaghetti have the same blessed resistance to ill treatment, and after several days unheeded in the icebox, can be steamed and shaped into more-than-acceptable companions to good meals.

One very simple casserole, which is delicious with baked ham, is made of lightly boiled noodles tossed with plenty of salt and pepper and one can of mushroom pieces that have been well browned in butter or good oil. You can put a few crumbs on the top if you like them [. . . or a crumbled handful of angel-hairs, finer than vermicelli, toasted nut-brown in a dry pan].

Any of these starches . . . *pastasciutti*, rices, potatoes . . . can be good alone, heated [Here I plainly mean "warmed over," the second or even third time. The tricks are to cook more than is needed for one meal, and to cook *lightly* and not to a starchy mush. Such leftovers are excellent fried, the way the Chinese treat rice.] and then stirred in a double boiler with butter, paprika, a little garlic if you like it, and a generous sprinkling of whatever chopped fresh herbs you have at hand. The garlic should be taken out of the butter before the rest is added.

Spaghetti, one of the most misunderstood simple foods in the world, can be one of the best when it is properly treated. It should in the first place be good, and fresh, and made with honest semolina flour so that it is hard and horny when uncooked, and firm, clean, smooth when it comes from the pot.

It should be cooked in a large quantity of salty boiling water, and stirred often. After about twenty minutes it should be tested several times by pressing a piece between your thumb and finger, so that it will not be too done and soft and soggy. When it is *almost* tender, run a little cold water into the pot to stop the cooking, and then drain it thoroughly so as not to spoil whatever sauce is coupled with it.

The next most important thing is to serve it while it is hot and at its peak of texture. If you like it as I do, in its simplest form, have a hot casserole with a generous amount of fresh melted butter in it. Pour in the spaghetti, which is of course in its original long strands, swirl it around a few times, and rush it to the table. There, on hot plates, let your guests eat it loaded as they will with more butter, salt and fresh pepper, and grated dry cheese of the Parmesan type. Salad or fruit and a plenitude of thin red wine makes this a perfect meal.

If you like a sauce with your spaghetti or any of the fifty children such as vermicelli, orzi, pennini, you can concoct just about such a brew as your fancy calls for—remembering always that mushrooms and tomato sauce and what herbs you can find should be a kindly part of it.

It is good to remember never to use flour in such a sauce, nor a canned tomato soup, but always let the canned or fresh tomato thicken by itself. Another important thing is to have the sauce ready before you cook the paste, and in the same way to have your guests ready to eat it before you serve the dish, since once cooked and mingled it cannot wait. The sauce, of course, can be prepared many hours before you want it, but if by any chance you must serve the paste long after it is cooked, drain it and wash it thoroughly before it is quite done, and then heat it quickly in boiling water before serving it.

Always have a well-heated and generous platter ready for the paste and the sauce, which should either be mixed lightly together just before serving or shaped into a filled mound which can be tossed and spooned together as it is given to each person. Grated cheese should be served separately.

One of the best sauces for spaghetti is, or was, a favorite one in Naples, and it is so simple and satisfying that even confirmed meat-eaters forget their conditioned hungers when they have it. (It is agreeably economical, too.)

Napolitana Sauce for Spaghetti

5	tablespoons olive oil (or decent substitute, if any)	½	green pepper
2	cloves garlic	2	cups tomato sauce (2 small cans)
1	sweet onion		salt, pepper
1	carrot	3	tablespoons herbs

Mince the garlic, onion, carrot, and pepper into the oil. Cook, stirring gently, for 10 minutes. Add the tomato sauce and the seasoning and herbs, such as chopped marjoram and thyme and parsley. Cook slowly for about 20 minutes, stirring often. Serve with hot paste and grated cheese.

Probably the nearest thing to polenta our country can lay claim to is Southern spoon bread, which is a dainty and more expensive and at the same time more limited dish than its Italian ancestor. It is very good indeed, as any authentic Carolina cook, past, present, or future, will be glad to prove to you. It can be served, delicate and steaming, with chicken or whatever casserole you may have. It can even act as backbone for a dishful of leftover gravy or sauce, to which you have probably added a few canned mushrooms and some fresh herbs and sherry. [I often use olives in such brews, the black pitted medium or small size, halved or quartered. It is best to toss them and the mushrooms thoroughly in a little oil or butter, then add the herbs, then the leftover sauce, and finally the sherry. Everybody stays unquestioning and pleased, especially olive-loathers, of whom there are many.]

Southern Spoon Bread

2	*cups cornmeal*	3	*large tablespoons butter, melted*
1½	*cups sweet milk*		
2	*cups boiling water*	3	*eggs*
1	*teaspoon salt*		

Sift the meal three times and mix until it is smooth into the boiling water. Add the melted butter and salt, and thin with the milk.

Separate the eggs, and beat until light, folding first the yolks and then the whites into the batter. Pour into a buttered baking dish, bake about 30 minutes in a moderate oven (350°), and serve in its dish.

Polenta, in contrast to this somewhat ephemeral and ladylike dish, is a sturdy, forthright, almost truculent mixture, the kind that has survived centuries of loving obedience from hungry simple peoples. It is really cornmeal mush, nothing more. But it is dressed for the fair, in its most exciting clothes, and it can be the mainstay of a poor family's nourishment or the central dish of a buffet supper for twenty jaded literary critics with equal nonchalance. [One of the most painful things about X's annotating X is a sentence like this. ". . . with equal nonchalance" should follow the phrase "and it can." It is apparently more obvious to X now than it was in 1942. X blushes.]

It should be prepared just before it is to be served, and the plates should be hot, for like all starches it chills quickly and loses some of its good nutlike taste as it does so. It can be cooked for about one hour in a thick iron pot, and stirred often with a wooden paddle. It will form a crust inside the pot, which should not be disturbed nor permitted to burn. Or it can cook about three hours in a double boiler without stirring. The first method is plainly quicker, but needs more attention. If the polenta becomes too thick, add more water.

The sauce for it, which can be practically anything you like as long as it is dark and aromatic with herbs and filled with succulent morsels of mushrooms and olives and whatever else you want, can have beef in it or chicken or even shellfish, according to your pocketbook. Or it can stand on its own feet, as I have often proved, without any assistance from flesh, fowl, or fish. Make it the day before you use it, if you want to.

The main thing to remember, probably, is that polenta is not ordinary cornmeal, but a much coarser "grind" that can be bought in any Italian grocery store, or in most large markets.

Polenta

3 cups cold water	(1 cup diced Monterey or
3 cups boiling water	mild goat cheese; optional
2 cups polenta meal	but good)
2 teaspoons salt	grated Parmesan-type cheese

Stir the meal gradually with the cold water to form a smooth mixture. Slowly add it to the boiling salted water, stirring constantly to prevent lumps. If in a double boiler, cook without further stirring for three hours. If in a heavy iron pot, stir gently now and then for an hour with a wooden paddle, taking care not to disturb the crust that will form against the pot.

The polenta should be about the consistency of spoon bread when done. If too thick, add more hot water.

Stir in the cubed cheese at the last if desired. Then shape into a mound and cover with grated cheese, to be served separately with whatever sauce is desired. Or make into a ring around the sauce on one plate.

A Beef Sauce for Polenta

¼ cup olive or other good oil	1 whole clove
1 large onion, chopped	2 peppercorns
1 clove garlic, minced	salt and herbs to taste
1 cup chopped celery	½ cup dried mushrooms
1 carrot, sliced thin	1 cup hot water
1 large can solid-pack tomatoes	2½ pounds beef cut into 1-inch cubes
1 bayleaf	

[I think this is too much beef, and in too large pieces. I would settle for half the quantity, cut or chopped into much smaller morsels. And I have decided that a twig of fresh or dried rosemary is a happy herb to add and then fish out at the last. And I like green pepper, in slivers or squares.]

Sauté the onion, garlic, carrot, and celery in the oil until they are relaxed and beginning to be brown. Add the tomatoes, spices, and herbs (thyme, marjoram, basil).

Soak the mushrooms in hot water until tender. Cut into small pieces, strain the water, and add it all to the sauce. Cover, and let simmer for 3 to 4 hours.

Brown the beef in a little fat or oil. Add a little boiling water or stock and let simmer until tender. Add to the sauce about 1 hour before serving, so that the two may marry their flavors.

Serve in a large bowl, to be poured [ladled is a better word here] over the sliced polenta on each plate.

A sauce made with chicken is less strongly seasoned. One with hare is better if a good dry wine is used instead of water, as indeed any can be, according to your tastes and prejudices. [If made with cooked shrimps, they should be added about ten minutes before time to serve the whole. Little clams, oysters, or shrimps, either raw and shucked or raw and frozen (and, of course, shucked!), should be simmered in butter until they curl and then added just before serving. And so on . . . a combination of common sense and courage is indicated!]

Polenta is one of those ageless culinary lords, like bread. It has sprung from the hunger of mankind, and without apparent effort has always carried with it a feeling of strength and dignity and well-being.

It costs little to prepare, if there is little to spend, or it can be extravagantly, opulently odorous with wines and such. It can be made doggedly, with one ear cocked for the old wolf's sniffing under the door, or it can be turned out as a well-nourished gesture to other simpler days. But no matter what conceits it may be decked with, its fundamental simplicity survives, to comfort our souls as well as our bellies, the way a good solid fugue does, or a warm morning in spring.

How to Be Content
with a Vegetable Love

> If he's content with a vegetable love which would certainly
>   not suit me,
> Why, what a most particularly pure young man this pure,
>   young man must be!
>
> *Patience,* W. S. GILBERT

Purity may have something to do with a vegetable love, but is
almost certain to have nothing to do with a love of vegetables,
since *petits pois à la Française* have been known to appeal to the
lowest as well as the loftiest emotions of at least one hardened
sinner.

[There is, of course, an excellent recipe for this naive and delicate dish in Escoffier and many another cookbook. And like
many another cook I seldom pay any attention to it. Instead I fit
the ways to the means: I use uniformly mediocre frozen peas in
preference to unpredictably uneven market peas, if I cannot
pick my own from a now vanished garden. If I have good garden shallots or onions I use them. If I have my own lettuces I am
happiest, but I have often settled, with silent resignation, for a
small tight head of tasteless "Alaska" (which is insultingly

called Los Angeles Lettuce in salad-happy San Francisco!). I use salted butter, for want of the sweet. And so on and so on. My *petits pois* more-or-less *à la Française* always please me . . . as long as I manage not to have the telephone ring at the moment they should be done, and let them turn pale or puckered.

Petits Pois à la Française

½ cup water	2 pounds peas
1 head lettuce	¼ pound good butter
6 green onions	salt, fresh pepper
handful of parsley	

Put water in heavy casserole or pot; shred lettuce coarsely into it; add onions split and cut in 2-inch pieces, using tops; chop parsley and add. Put peas on this bed, and put chunk of butter on top. Cover tightly and bring slowly to boil, shaking now and then. Lower heat, let cook for about 5 minutes, and serve at once, mixing all well together and seasoning to taste. There should be almost no liquid. More butter can be added at the last if it seems desirable.]

What can be said about vegetables as a form of gastronomical entertainment is best said simply, since once past the basic behavior, all such recipes depend on you and what you need.

Almost all vegetables are good, although there is some doubt still about parsnips (which I share). [I am no longer doubtful. I *know*. And rutabaga has joined the exclusive group.]

All of them whether tender or hard, thick-skinned or thin, die when they are peeled . . . even as you and I. Therefore it is better to cook them always in their skins, at least until they are partly done, and then prepare them as you had planned.

With the exception of cabbage, and very strong tough and probably inedible turnips, vegetables should be cooked in as little water as possible. [I now know that I can cook quartered cabbage in a cup of water, and shredded cabbage in no water at all but instead a pat of butter or a little good fat or oil. As for the turnips I describe so bluntly . . . why bother?] Steam cookers are good, or the new pressure cookers that are so economical if you can afford to buy them at all.

When what is left of the steam and water is not to be used as a sauce, with a little butter stirred into it, it should be poured into a bottle and kept in the icebox. Any such juices you have can be mixed together, and then shaken before they are used.

And used they will be: in clear soups, as stock in sauces, as a quick pickup when you are tired (ice-cold with a little lemon juice or an equal part of tomato juice). The natural salts from all the different vegetables will make a pungent palatable stock, usually, without any salt or pepper.

The same is true of any juices from canned vegetables: they should *never* be thrown away, but drained with due respect for their value into the stock-bottle, along with the rest of the essences.

Canned vegetables are usually good, and often have more of the all-necessary vitamins and minerals in them than do the same vegetables cooked at home. This is mostly true because they are cooked within the can, and therefore lose none of their attributes. Also, the wily packers, anxious to build up the weight of each tin, use as much water as they dare, which by the time it gets to you is beautifully rich and full of flavor.

Frozen vegetables are very good. The directions on the package should be followed carefully, except that usually even less time is needed than they say, to cook the peas or beans or corn to perfection.

For that matter *no* vegetable should be cooked as long as you think. Of course this depends a little on altitude and fuel and pot, but in general it is true that vegetables are almost always overcooked.

Some people use salt in the water, but for myself I prefer to add whatever seasoning I want just at the last. The vegetables seem tenderer, and the flavor of sweet butter and freshly ground pepper is more characterful.

This is not the case, naturally, with fresh herbs: they should be put in right at the beginning, tied in a bundle if you want to remove them before serving. [My taste has changed. Some herbs, but not all, should be cooked at length. Rosemary, for instance, can stew for a long time in a chicken pot or a saucepan. So can thyme or bay. But marjoram, parsley, anise . . . I put them in at the last. It is apparently a question of current favor as well as flavor!] The possibilities of their flavors, blended or alone, are limitless: the basils, the marjorams, thyme, the sages, mint, anise . . . what delights they conjure, if you want them to!

It is possible, and also practical, to buy vegetables once or twice a week at a big market, and prepare them all at once. [This is indeed a practical idea, but I do not approve of it in theory. The gastronomical values of most vegetables do dwindle with time.] It is a rather long but restful job, to wash and cut and chop and then cook what you will want for the next few days, and there is something more than satisfying in the beautiful crisp piles on your drain-board.

You should undercook everything, and then when it is cool put it in the icebox, in covered dishes, if it has a strong flavor like cauliflower. You will feel good, looking into the box and seeing several meals practically ready to eat. You can think of simple things for one dish, like hot buttered crumbs poured over the cauliflower, or a can of beansprouts mixed with some chopped pepper and the green beans.

Or you can plan a grand hash at the end of the week, of every vegetable that is left, tossed in a skillet with some chopped bacon and tomatoes. Or a frittata, made with eggs. Or a delicately heartening salad, made in a bowl the way you used to see it in Venice, the cooked and the raw entwined in an exciting marriage. [One of the most happily ubiquitous of cooked vegetables is the new potato, preferably pink-skinned and tiny. In salads it is wonderful. Hot, combined with peas or green beans or broiled mushrooms or or or, it is heavenly. Alone, in a mist of sweet butter, it is divine. And there is no right word in my lexicon for new potatoes very cold, in their skins of course, with a bowl of thick sour cream alongside to dunk them in.]

There are many ways to love a vegetable. The most sensible way is to love it well-treated. Then you can eat it with the comfortable knowledge that you will be a better man for it, in your spirit and your body too, and will never have to worry about your own love being vegetable.

How to
Make a Great Show

By economy and good management, by a sparing use of
ready money, and by paying scarcely anybody, people can
manage, for a time at least, to make a great show with very
little means.

Vanity Fair, THACKERAY

In spite of the present flurry of interest in gastronomical and
household economy, brought on by the first realization of war
here at home, not even the most excited magazine advises quite
such a philosophy as was practiced by Thackeray's Becky. Her
attitude was cynical, and probably too empty of that slight
touch of sentiment that almost every woman enjoys in her re-
lations with the world. For without sentiment, how else could
you explain some of the incredible suggestions for economy offered in the backs of cookbooks for the last hundred years, even
unto 1925?

I am sure that a strong but secret desire to impress your
mother-in-law, or perhaps your husband or growing daughter,
with your brave martyrdom and gallantry, is all that would

make you follow most of the "helpful hints," or what are called in one astonishing English book, "Wrinkles for the Cook."

Does the fuel problem seem grim and thin? Here are some suggestions that sound touched with a kind of sordid whimsy until you try them. Then they really work, and make you feel noble and brave at the same time.

Get one package of fireclay from a fuel-man, and mix it into a stiff paste with water. Make it into balls about the size of oranges (or a little smaller if you are thinking of California navels). Dry them in the oven: you are having baked potatoes and a potroast anyway that night. Leave them overnight in the cooling oven if you can, and when they seem dry put them into the fire.

That is all. They get red-hot, and give off a lot of heat, and if you treat them gently with the poker and when you are cleaning the hearth, they will last "for ages," as the book rather naively puts it. Also, somewhat naively, they are called Hot Spots!

Or if you don't want to muck around in wet fireclay, put an empty tin can or two in the center of your burning fire . . . if you still have any tin cans. It will last three or four days, and will send off a surprising lot of heat that apparently was going up the chimney before.

And you can make one burner of a gas stove heat about four pots if you put a twelve-inch square of sheet-iron over it and *if* you have an old-fashioned stove. (This "hint" smacks definitely of 1897, when it was published.) A modern stove with its burners prettily embedded in large spaces of white enamel would be ruined beyond hope, probably, after any such attempt at economy.

A thousand other suggestions for saving money are as plainly dated, in most of the books. How many women now care about knowing how to clean horsehair cushions, or what to do with moulting feather beds . . . or even how to "treat an Art-Work Brass Bed"? (Except as a conversational gambit at a cocktail party.)

In almost every list, which is usually at the back of the volume, just before the index, and is called everything from "Large Helps in Little Hints" to "Experientia Docet," there is at least one tip about how to cure hiccups. This seems strange, or perhaps it is merely a tactless admission that some of the recipes preceding it are none too digestible.

"In Case of Fire" is another old faithful, and it advises everything for putting out the blaze, from throwing one pound of sulphur up the chimney to making complicated liquids that must be stored in a cool dark cellar . . . to putting on plenty of water.

Beauty, as it should be, is another problem that is fairly well covered in the hints. To Whiten the Arms, A Lotion to Remove Freckles, A Remedy for Tender Feet or Fingertips . . . how they all bring back a faint but heady memory of the great belles, and heavy velvet swags, and pink candle-shades and cigars-with-the-port!

But when the belles grew less so, and their hair a little thin at the sides of the pompadours, did they really rub their scalps with onion juice several times a week? Did they (*could* they?) put gasoline liberally on their heads daily and coconut oil three times a week, if their gilded tresses finally began to fall in earnest?

Or did they retire to their boudoirs, read a hint entitled, starkly, Nervous Breakdown, and proceed to develop all its carefully detailed phenomena?

Some of the recipes for family necessities given in these collections are really useful, however, like the one called A Pleasant Tooth Wash, which was discovered several months ago by a woman with five children who gargled, swished, and spat their way through countless quarts of expensive antiseptic solutions with Gargantuan abandon.

It is a formula suggested by a book printed during the first World War, when alcohol in England was almost as dear and as difficult to find as it will soon be in America in the second, and it is an agreeable and cheap and generally adequate substitute for the various bottled washes we have been educated to consider an intrinsic part of our daily toilets.

Mouth Wash

2 *ounces borax*	1 *teaspoon tincture of myrrh*
1 *quart hot water*	1 *teaspoon spirits of camphor*

Dissolve the borax in very hot water. When it has cooled, add the other ingredients and bottle. (A little pink coloring can be added if your children demand it.)

There are many tooth powders that can be made at the cost of a few cents, and which after the first shock are as good as the commercial ones, if not quite so suave and sweet. Once when I was hardup (to make a definite understatement), I used a mixture of equal parts of baking soda and common salt, mixed in a mason jar with a few drops of peppermint to take off the curse, or most of it. [It was horrible. I still remember it with revulsion, and if I had to depend on it again would prefer to use a willow twig, or let my teeth crumble.]

And then there is a recipe in one of the older cookbooks that says to mix equal parts of castile soap, powdered orris root, and precipitated chalk. I am unable to see castile soap in anything but uneven and sharp-edged bilious cakes, in my mind's eye, and on mature consideration would have none of this prescription, since I think it could be almost as disagreeable as it sounds.

And soap: it probably will be harder in wartime than you yet realize. English women, the papers whisper, are putting special strainers in their kitchen drains to catch all the grease . . . an ugly picture but perhaps not much less so than one conjured by this recipe:

Monkey Soap

Mix together equal parts of soft soap, bath brick, and whiting. Make into convenient cakes. Dry slowly.

If you want to be clean and still keep at least part of the skin where it should be on your body, the following recipe is perhaps more merciful:

To Make Soap

5 pounds melted grease (fats not fit for food)	1 teaspoon salt
	2 tablespoons sugar
1 one-pound can lye	½ cup cold water
1 quart cold water	¼ cup ammonia
3 teaspoons borax	

Dissolve the lye in cold water and let cool. Then add the fat slowly, stirring constantly. Mix the other ingredients together and add to the first mixture. Stir the whole until thick and light in color. Pour into a pan lined with cloth, and mark into pieces before the soap becomes hard. When it is hard, break apart and pile so that it will dry thoroughly.

There are many variants of this basic rule, which is purely functional and looks ugly and smells worse. It is better than nothing, however—*much better*, if you agree that cleanliness runs a close second to godliness. [To a friend in England, a beautiful and quite ungodly woman but very clean, I send regularly a package containing about five kinds of plain good soap: powdered, flaked, unperfumed in cakes. She loves it more than orchids.]

There is one recipe, again from an English book, which has puzzled me for a long time and which need only be read by some master of the straight face to sound like the most involved suggestion. It talks about one thing, but even my dazed mind feels that it wishes to talk about another and at the same time spare the delicate feelings of true ladies born-and-bred.

To Cure Bruised Withers

Ladies who ride astride on horseback may be glad to know of the following remedy. . . . Lay on the sore or bruised part a damp sod of earth, about two inches thick, mold side next to the horse. It should be about two inches larger than the affected part. Fasten on under the night sheet and roller. Leave it on all night.

You can use tea leaves (to skip with discreet haste to another field) in an alarming number of ways after they have fulfilled their natural function of making tea. They are fine for keeping down the dust on Aubusson carpets, the books say . . . or any kind of carpets at all. They make it easier to clean out a fireplace without getting ash all over everything. They are also good to clean the insides of water bottles, the books say again, but it is hard to understand why the insides of water bottles should be dirty with anything but water anyway. [I evidently did not know much about water in 1942! I have since discovered that nothing can make worse stains, and that the best way to keep bottles sparkling is to use something like Ke-Nu in them. Probably feeding two babies has added to my knowledge!]

You can also steep them and tint lace with them, thank God.

And to sum up the whole atmosphere of economy as preached, if not always practiced, in the section of cookbooks of another generation than this one (again we can give praise!), here is a hint that can be found in at least five volumes, the first edited in 1840-something, and the last published by the Ladies of the Saint Matthias Guild of a Far West church in 19—yes, 19, not 18—25. It reads, in each version, almost exactly like this, and should be a lesson to us all:

To Stuff Pincushions

Coffee grounds, well steeped and dried, make an excellent stuffing. They are economical and keep the needles and pins from wasteful rust, and will not pack down.

Pax Vobiscum.

How to
Have a Sleek Pelt

I love little pussy!
Her coat is so warm!
And if I don't hurt her
She'll do me no harm
JOHN SEBASTIAN DOE

This optimistic jingle has probably done more to exasperate embryonic poets than any other in the English language. Not only is it sanctimonious and sticky; it has an impossible rhyme. The last word should be *horm*, unless you speak in German dialect; and what is *horm*? Horm might be a new kind of sandwich spread, or a revitalizing tonic, but it is certainly not what Pussy will do to you. Pussy will and can do a lot of other things to you, though. (Pussy is an insipid name, associated in my mind for some thirty years with the glazed pink-and-white blue-eyed mug of the unhealthily plump little girl whose picture illustrated the nursery jingle. It will be more agreeable, I think, to assume that you have a cat named Blackberry, and a dog named P'ing Cho Fung by the Kennel Association and Butch by you.)

Blackberry and Butch, then, can cause you a lot of extra

worry, now that men have decided to live by the sword again, temporarily.

They and other furry creatures are among the first to suffer, like the meek. The thought of all the fine shining cows crying in agony to be milked along the roads of France and Belgium, while the hungry people fled past them, is an ugly one. And at the beginning of this war, it was a sorrowful idea in England that pets should not drink and eat the precious food, nor breathe the invaluable cellar air that their human masters might use. In Honolulu, on another island, the same thoughtless instinct rose in the first days of war, and the civilians were urged not to waste food on pets.

There is one eccentric and wealthy old lady in Cornwall, the kind who is often the victim in mystery stories, who was stoned in 1940 because she had refused to kill her cat and her terrier. Moreover, she had turned her cellars and her air-raid shelter into a haven for every pet she could rescue from the panicky village. That seemed terrible to the people, to feed and protect brute-beasts while little children were bombed and might be hungry too. The old lady was most unpopular, in 1940.

But in 1941 she was not. By then the rats and mice were scampering prolifically and plumply through many another village than hers, and contrary to centuries of habit, people beamed instead of groaned when they saw an *enceinte* alley cat, or heard a terrier ratting in the barn. All the eccentric old ladies and the others who from sentiment or coolheadedness had refused to do away with their Butches and Blackberries were enhaloed, and it was confessed, as it soon must be in any beleaguered place, that there are worse things than sharing what food there is with old friends, even supposedly soulless ones.

It is of course harder and more expensive to feed animals in wartime. It takes more thought and planning, just as with humans.

Dogs are more of a problem than cats, since they are believed to be carnivorous and have small scope to exercise that nature, fortunately for us. (One of the handsomest I ever saw, though, with a pelt like a Russian opera-singer's winter overcoat, was a vegetarian from birth . . . and a police dog at that!) They must be fed with more expense, if not more care, than the ordinary house-cat . . . who if she's worth her salt will do a bit of mousing, war or no war, and can fend for herself with the inspiration of a good saucer of milk now and then, and a comforting bite from the kitchen leftovers. [Most cats and many dogs appreciate dainty tidbits, and I always share my scraps with my current feline companion. She and I nibble at the same food, from different dishes and physical levels, and feel companionable. It is another good argument for the spiritual value of leftovers, with their accumulated savor.]

Dogs, like men, can grow lean in wartime with no great danger and perhaps some good, and like men they will show by their outsides how their simpler diet agrees with them. If their eyes are dull, and their fur is lifeless and thin, and their nails are cracked, and they seem easy prey to drifting disease clouds, then they are malnourished just as surely as any sad wretch kept alive in a concentration camp on thin soup and bread.

There are countless little books and pamphlets, most of them published by pet-food packers, to tell you how to feed your dog correctly. In spite of their eagerness to prove that Rex-O or Pussy-Purr-More is the only correct food, most of them agree that a fairly ideal diet for a dog should consist roughly of one-third meat, one-third vegetable, and one-third starch. This, with variations according to the individual, is basically man's diet too!

In time of war, when eating becomes less of a gastronomic exercise and more a part of a determined will-to-live, you can nourish yourself and Butch on the same schedule, and do harm to neither of you. The sludge I write about in the chapter on how to keep alive is, in my experience, the finest all-in-one diet for any normal dog or cat alive.

It can be made more coarsely, chopped instead of ground, for big animals whose guts are longer and stronger than a terrier's or a Peke's. It should always be broken up nicely in the dish (it gets very solid when cool), but should never be made soupy with additional liquid. If possible it should be warmed a little in cold weather. And one meal of it a day will keep any type of dog I have known in such top form that veterinarians will blink with jealousy.

Another thing to give Butch, and Blackberry too, is an occasional nibble of fresh yeast. It seems to make their coats even finer, and their mouths sweeter. They can have a quarter- or a half-cake at a time, maybe once or twice a week. You can see that it is no great addition to the budget, and it is well worth it.

Most of the reputable canned foods are all right, especially if they are given only occasionally as a treat (which is also easier on the pocketbook). They can be mixed with sludge, to go farther.

A raw egg, now and then, for your pets is a good investment, too. [My own offspring down an occasional raw yolk from its half-shell, and I am convinced that their sleek pelts are the sleeker for it . . . and their palates the happier!] It should be stirred into milk or sludge, since it is rather slithery to lap up, I imagine.

If you give canned milk, always dilute it, preferably with tomato juice or the juices you have saved for your own use from canned or cooked vegetables. Needless to say, your animals need vitamins and minerals just as you do, and what you have you should share with them as long as you assume the responsibility of keeping them alive at all.

Myself, I have always said (and practiced) [This still stands, as does the whole chapter.] that I would never give a dog or a cat what I would not eat myself. Sometimes it has been hard to discard a whole can of some new recommended food, which when I opened it sent out such a stink of old meat and spurious seasoning that I knew I could never swallow the trial bite of it.

In reverse, though, it is fairly safe to say that what neither Blackberry nor Butch will touch is no fit food for you. For instance, canned luncheon meat, which resembles dog food in many ways, except that it is more expensive: if neither animal enjoys a bite of it, you can count on its being too salty or too impossibly pink and healthy with a mass of preservatives that will parch your tongue and burn your innards.

Once, in a madcap mood indeed, I bought a generous tin of sliced smoked salmon from Poland. I made a beautiful platter of it for an hors d'œuvre, and then, feeling magnanimous, put one slice on a plate for Bazeine, the current Blackberry.

He sniffed it, backed away as if it had snapped at him, and with a reproachful glare at me disappeared for two days. Which is almost what happened with the humans a little later, since I couldn't bring myself to throw away fifteen francs, and served the salmon in spite of Bazeine's blunt hint.

The next morning I made a little pile of all the beautiful paper-thin bright orange slices, and carried them mournfully down through the vineyard to the compost pit. They looked gay and still delectable, there on top of all the vegetable trimmings and dead flowers.

Months later, when I was cleaning away the leaves of a magnificent melon that grew from a seed in the pit and covered it for a whole summer, I saw the smoked salmon again.

It sat just where I had placed it, on top of all the dead vegetation. The sun had not faded its gay color, and snow and wind and rain had not warped its oily squareness. Birds had ignored it, or flown away in fright perhaps, and even the wise ants had left it inviolate.

Finally the pit was covered with earth, and soon lush wild flowers grew where it had been. But I have a feeling sometimes that if I ever get back to that meadow below the vineyard in Switzerland, the strange frightful square of bright orange salmon will have worked its way up through the ground and the roots and be lying there, a deathless taunt to my gastronomic snobbism and the time I refused to take a cat's advice. [For one of the few times in the past thirty-odd years I am pleased with something I have written. I think this is a good chapter.]

How to
Comfort Sorrow

I'll make her a pudding, and a pudding she'll like, too. . . .
Many a one has been comforted in their sorrow by seeing a
good dish come upon the table.

Cranford, MRS. GASKELL

There are those of us, and perhaps it is a good sign, who hold
that puddings are fit food for babes and dodderers and such mis-
fortunes with few teeth and less esthetic taste. Others, and
who is to say whether they are right or not, would agree with
Cranford's quaint character that a pudding can be a fine heartwarming thing indeed, in times of sorrow.

In times of war, however, puddings can be pesky nuisances.
If you are cooking for people who feel that because they ate
some such sweet desserts once a day when they were young,
they must perforce eat them once a day when they are middle-
aged and working like everything to save democracy, you will
be hard put to it to make their prejudices fit your food bill. Eggs
and cream and cinnamon, not to mention fuel needed for long
slow bakings, have suddenly become rare and precious things
to be used cunningly for a whole meal or a weekly treat, not as
the routine and unctuous final fillip to a prewar dinner.

In England now, many of the gruesome gastronomical pixies of the last unpleasantness have come into the open again, and you can buy powdered War-Egg-O ("Housewives . . . stir in a bit of water and treat your family *tonight* to a tempting custard sauce!") and even something called Nooeg, which is guaranteed to contain no egg at all, but will please your friends with its rich delightful smoothness ("upon tinned fruits").

These doubtful triumphs of science over human hunger are perhaps less dreadful to the English than to us, for in spite of our national appetite for pink gelatine puddings, we have never been as thoroughly under the yoke of Bird's Custard Sauce as our allies. [This situation no longer obtains. We not only buy incredible quantities of packaged American puddings, but we can now, oh, happy people, get *Bird's* in our "better" groceries!] Let us hope, without malice, that Nooeg stays on the right side of the Atlantic.

For those who must have some "shapeless nothing in a dish," war or no war, at the end of every nighttime meal, the easiest and cheapest (and most pitying) answer is the boxed ready-prepared gelatine dessert. It is well advertised and even well thought of in some circles. Therefore, let us dismiss both it and its admirers from our thoughts.

Probably one of the best ends to a supper is nothing at all. If the food has been simple, plentiful, and well prepared; if there has been time to eat it quietly, with a friend or two; if the wine or beer or water has been good: then, more often than not, most people will choose to leave it so, with perhaps a little cup of coffee for their souls' sake.

Another fine thing for the soul, after a meal in the evening, is one of those herbal teas that French people used to call *tisanes*. [Serving a *tisane* before bedtime may sound affected, but very few people are anything but pleased by one, if also somewhat startled.] They are simply hot water poured over a few dried leaves of mint or verbena or lime flowers or camomile. They can be drunk with or without sugar, and a twist of lemon can be added. They smooth out wrinkles in your mind miraculously, and make you sleep, with sweet dreams, too.

So thoroughly do even the most sophisticated of gastronmists believe in the magic of *tisanes*, that the following recipe was given only a few years ago with complete seriousness by the Vicomte de Mauduit:

Infusion of Ladies' Slipper Root

Last thing at night drink an infusion made of ladies' slipper root. Then under your pillow case place a mixed bouquet of this root and skullcap, which you have previously dried in the oven. This is a permanent *cure for sleeplessness.*

If you have supped well, for instance, on ham baked with apples and sweet potatoes and a green salad, you will probably agree that the best possible ending to such a savorous meal is a bowl of walnuts that have been roasting in their shells in the hot oven while you ate. Coffee is fine with them, but a glass of port is even better . . . or ordinary red wine.

Coffee, by the way, is one thing which cannot be made skimpily. If you are going to economize with it, do so by using it less often, but never by trying to make it with less coffee and cooking it longer. Almost any good grocery store sells a very inexpensive, moderately well-roasted brand of coffee in the grain, which you can have ground to your taste in half-pound lots, so that it is used before it grows too stale. (Or if you are lucky you can grind it yourself as you need it, in your nice old-fashioned coffee mill or your nice new-fashioned electric grinder.) This bulk coffee costs about half the price of tinned brands, and is good.

If you use Sanka or Kaffee Hag, you can do it with a clear conscience and a certain malicious pleasure in the number of people you fool, if you make it with a generous hand: two tablespoonfuls to the cup.

And any coffee, emasculated or not, is better than perfect if it is made with chicory. It can be bought in this country, in spite of what many stubborn repatriated gourmets say, in convenient little brown tablets. It is cheap and easy to use, and not only improves the flavor of no matter what brand of coffee, but with a certain amount of judicious experimenting can be made to make a pound go much further than it is meant to by the merchants. [There is a good "Italian over-roast" brand of canned coffee now generally obtainable. I am sorry to say that the little chicory tablets seem to have disappeared, and that they are a gastronomical loss that I am apparently alone in feeling!]

Coffee, when it is brewed intelligently, is a perfect accompaniment to any dessert, whether it be a Soufflé au Grand Marnier or a bowl of frost-whipped Winesap apples, crisp and juicy. It is good, too, with a piece of fruity cake, and here is a recipe for one that is foolproof to concoct, and guaranteed to make the wolf take at least two steps back, instead of one step nearer.

It is a remnant of the last war, and although I remember liking it so much that I dreamed about it at night [Unimportant note: I mentioned this with some embarrassment on page 22. Now I dream of caviar. And if I should live so long, will it be of gruel and milksops?] like all the other children who ate it, I can't remember that it was ever called anything more appetizing than

War Cake

½ cup shortening (bacon grease can be used, because of the spices that hide its taste)	1 cup sugar, brown or white 1 cup water

1 *teaspoon cinnamon*
1 *teaspoon other spices . . .
   cloves, mace, ginger, etc.*
1 *cup chopped raisins or other
   dried fruits . . . prunes,
   figs, etc.*

2 *cups flour, white or whole
   wheat*
¼ *teaspoon soda*
2 *teaspoons baking powder*

*Sift the flour, soda, and baking powder. Put all the other ingredients in
a pan, and bring to a boil. Cook 5 minutes. Cool thoroughly. Add the
sifted dry ingredients and mix well. Bake 45 minutes or until done in a
greased loaf-pan in a 325–350° oven.*

War cake can be made in muffin-tins, and baked more quickly,
but in a loaf it stays fresh longer. It is very good with a glass of
milk, I remember. (I am sure that I could live happily forever
without tasting it again. There are many things like that: you re-
call with astonishment and a kind of admiration some of the
things eaten with sensual delight at eight or eighteen, that
would be a gastronomical *auto da fé* for you at twenty-eight, or
fifty. But that does not mean that you were wrong so long ago.
War Cake says nothing to me now, but I know that it is an honest
cake, and one loved by hungry children. And I'm not ashamed
of having loved it . . . merely a little puzzled, and thankful that
I am no longer eight.)

Another good cake, to eat plain with coffee, or frosted with a
covering of cream cheese and powdered sugar and a little rum if
possible, is

Tomato Soup Cake

3 *tablespoons butter or
   shortening*
1 *cup sugar*
1 *teaspoon soda*

1 *teaspoon cinnamon*
1 *teaspoon nutmeg, ginger,
   cloves mixed*

| 1 can tomato soup | 1½ cups raisins, nuts, chopped |
| 2 cups flour | figs, what you will |

Cream butter, add the sugar, and blend thoroughly. Add the soda to the soup, stirring well, and add this alternately to the first mixture with the flour and spices sifted together. Stir well, and bake in a pan or loaf-tin at 325°.

This is a pleasant cake, which keeps well and puzzles people who ask what kind it is. It can be made in a moderate oven while you are cooking other things, which is always sensible and makes you feel rather noble, in itself a small but valuable pleasure.

Another excellent way to use any space left from cooking meat or a casserole or anything that wants a moderate heat, is, as I have already argued, to make baked apples. They are good hot or cold, stuffed with raisins or with brown sugar. [Or mincemeat or leftover jam. Cannelloni (p. 107) are also a fine dessert made with jam.] They can make a whole supper, with plenty of hot buttered toast, or they can be the rather heavy but savory and wholesome dessert of a dinner, served with sour cream or my grandmother's recipe for Cinnamon Milk.

Baked Apples

| apples . . . almost any kind, although Deliciouses are delicious | cinnamon, nutmeg |
| brown sugar (1 tablespoon for each apple) | raisins, dates, leftover jam butter (optional) water |

Core the apples, and put in a baking dish. Fill each hole with the fruit or jam, and put a dab of butter on top if you want to. Mix the sugar with enough water to fill the dish almost to the top, and bake slowly until the apples are tender.

Cinnamon Milk
(For Baked Apples or Apple Dumplings)

1 *pint milk*	1 *tablespoon butter (optional)*
1 *teaspoon cinnamon or mixed*	
spices	

[Age makes me less ascetic, and the butter is no longer optional! And now I use creamy milk and add either 3 tablespoonfuls of brown sugar or about half that amount of good molasses. Other people like it better too!]

Heat milk in double boiler. Add spices (and butter). Pour into heated jug and serve like cream.

An easy and inexpensive hot dessert, if your oven is going anyway, is a shallow buttered casserole with a handful of gingersnaps [. . . or vanilla wafers or old sponge cake . . . and of course the fruit is well *drained*] in the bottom and a can of peaches on them. Put a little butter in each peach, sprinkle some nutmeg here and there, and if you feel lavish pour a little sherry into the dish. Broil, and serve with or without cream, which is better sour than sweet for most such tried temptations. [A more interesting variation is canned nectarine-halves in a shallow buttered dish, filled with leftover preserves, a little lump of butter, nutmeg if desired. I grill them for five minutes, and for company or fun pour a little dark rum over them and let it burn off at the table. No cream, of course.]

The recipe for my mother's gingerbread must be almost identical with the excellent one that comes out of a box. It is cheaper to make, if you have the time and the oven is going anyway. It sends out a fine friendly smell through the house and is so good that it usually disappears while it is still hot, which is too bad because it is so good cold.

Edith's Gingerbread

[. . . which I mentioned on page 21, I believe.]

¼ cup shortening	cloves and salt
¼ cup sugar	¾ cup boiling water
½ cup molasses	¼ teaspoon soda
½ teaspoon soda	1¼ cups flour
1 teaspoon cinnamon	1 teaspoon baking powder
1 teaspoon ginger	1 beaten egg

Cream the shortening and sugar. Sift the spices and flour and baking powder together. Beat the ½ teaspoon soda into the molasses until it is light and fluffy, and add to the shortening and sugar. Add the ¼ teaspoon soda to the boiling water, and then add it alternately with the sifted dry ingredients. Fold in the beaten egg when all is well mixed, pour into a greased and floured pan, and bake about 20 minutes, at 325°F. This mixture will seem much too thin to make a cake, but do not *increase the quantity of flour, as many doubting cooks have tried to do.*

Either of the following simple sauces is good with it, although myself I think unsalted butter, preferably pressed into little pats with a cow on one side and a daisy on the other, is the most fitting partner.

A Wine Sauce

[Another excellent sauce is made of equal parts of brown sugar, butter, and sherry, beaten together while it slowly melts, and kept hot, but never bubbling.]

¼ cup butter	1 cup sherry
¾ cup powdered sugar	nutmeg
½ cup hot water	

Cream the butter, add the sugar gradually, and cream well. Add the nutmeg. Stir in the hot water and add the wine.

A Hard Sauce

¼ cup butter (or vegetable shortening, I hate to admit)	2 tablespoons lemon juice salt
½ cup powdered sugar	(rum if you like it)

Beat until very fluffy. (Add ¼ cup chopped nuts if desired.) [Or shred-ded coconut or chopped candied fruits. I like it best without additions.] Chill in a bowl and serve with hot gingerbread or any other hot cake.

It is hard to know whether a gingerbread should rightly be called a pudding when it is eaten hot with a sauce over it. (I re-member pale squares of warm cakey tastelessness, covered limply with a film of lemon-tinted sauce, which were called Cottage Pudding at boarding school.) The following rule, al-though it sounds rather like a cake, makes a pleasant hot dessert that is definitely a pudding. It is called Date Delight, through no fault of mine.

Date Delight

¼ cup butter or shortening	⅔ cup milk
⅔ cup sugar	¼ cup flour
2 eggs	½ teaspoon salt
3 cups soft crumbs	2 teaspoons baking powder
2 cups chopped dates	⅛ teaspoon soda
1 teaspoon ginger	½ teaspoon cinnamon

Cream shortening, eggs, sugar, until fluffy. Add ⅓ crumbs, dates, and then the rest of the crumbs and milk alternately. Add the sifted dry in-gredients. Beat briskly one minute, and bake in a greased pan 1 hour at 325°. Serve warm with hard sauce flavored with rum.

This, you can see, is a heavy dish, and more expensive than many. It should be made the main point of a meal, with perhaps soup and a light green salad first. It is a winter thing, and men usually like it more than women do.

Another hearty dessert, which can be made of sweet potatoes or yams left from day before yesterday's supper, is

Sweet Potato Pudding

6 sweet potatoes	grated rind and juice from 1
6 tablespoons butter (or	lemon or 1 orange
vegetable shortening)	2 bananas (optional)
6 tablespoons brown sugar	cinnamon

Peel the cooked or baked potatoes and mash smooth. Add the melted butter and brown sugar, the lemon rind and juice, and beat thoroughly. Pour into a buttered casserole (lined, if you wish, with sliced bananas) [. . . or any other fruit: pineapple, peaches, apples]. Put more brown sugar and a little butter and cinnamon, if possible, over the top, and bake ½ hour at 325–350°.

Leftover rice is another thing that can be used almost as many ways as there are people to eat it. Some of them think it a crying shame to do more than put some brown sugar and rich milk over it, and let it speak for itself. Others, more complicated in their actions, like some such recipe as the following, which I got from a Swiss woman:

Rice and Spice

2 eggs	½ teaspoon cinnamon
2 cups milk	¼ teaspoon each nutmeg,
¾ cup raisins	ginger, salt
1¼ cups cooked rice	1 tablespoon powdered sugar
½ cup brown sugar	

Separate the whites and yolks of the eggs. Add to the yolks 2 tablespoons of the milk, and place the rest of it in a double boiler. Wash the raisins, put them in the milk, and cook about 15 minutes or until they are soft. Add the rice, cook five minutes more, then stir in the yolks, sugar, salt, and spices. Cook for 2 to 3 minutes, stirring well. Pour into the serving dish. Beat the whites, add the powdered sugar, spread on the pudding, and brown delicately in the oven. Serve very cold.

This recipe is a dainty one, and will surprise people who remember rice pudding from their childhood with some unwillingness. There are many others like it, finicky to make perhaps but inexpensive and pleasant if you like them at all. [I still remember a basically similar pudding, but almost as crisp as a cake, made by a Turkish friend when I was only vaguely past childhood. It was of cooked vermicelli baked slowly in an oiled shallow pan, with more oil and much more honey basted over it until it could absorb no more. Perhaps there was a spice in it. It made my teeth ache.]

[A much daintier dish than Rice and Spice is Riz à l'Impératrice . . . or so I can read and have too often been assured, by friend and relatives raised, perforce and/or willy-nilly, in luxury hotels from Budapest to Colorado Springs. It is a dessert of the *fin de siècle* , a costly trifle to be played with before the hothouse peach, the Bock y Panatela . . . and people of about my age who raced the corridors of the Ritzes and the Trois Couronnes three or four decades ago can eat it with a poignant nostalgia unknown to me, the California kid, the crude *auslander*. It seems like a balm, a tonic, to their weary palates. And it is, in spite of its bland intricacy, a very gentle dish . . . somewhat like a notorious actress who is still naive . . .

(This recipe I give in a sketchy way, a fleeting cock-snoot at the wolf still sniffing hungrily. It is obvious that a good creamy rice-pudding, tricked out with apricot jam and currant jelly and well chilled, could nobly serve the purpose of the elaborate classicism I now outline:)

Riz à l'Impératrice

Wash, parboil, and then drain 1 pound of the finest rice. Slowly bake it with a vanilla bean, 1 quart of boiled rich milk, 2 cups fine white sugar, ¼ pound fresh butter. Keep covered and do not stir. When still hot add gently the beaten yolks of 16 eggs (ah, that happy wolf . . . !) When cool add 1 cup minced candied fruits and 1 cup apricot jam, 1 pint thick English custard, and 1 pint whipped cream heavily flavored with Alsatian kirsch. Put a thick layer of red currant jelly in the bottom of a Bavarian-cream mold, pour the above cream upon it, and let it chill thoroughly. To serve, turn out so that the jelly runs down over the firm sides. (This last is what sets off the cautious fireworks of reminiscence in my stomach-weary contemporaries who lived on such fatuous delicacies rather than my own grandmother's "plain boiled rice with cream and sugar.")]

"The proof of the pudding is in the eating," it says in *Don Quixote*. I believe it, myself, and would as soon have a hollowed ring of cold cooked cereal, Roman Meal, or Wheatena of hallowed memory, with the hollow filled with grated maple sugar and a fat pot of cream waiting, as I would Cherries Jubilee. But then, in spite of Cervantes and a host of awesome authorities, I would rather have some ripe grapes or a little properly selected cheese than any of their artful messes. Or nothing . . . wolf or no wolf.

How to
Be a Wise Man

A wise man always eats well.
Chinese proverb

Every now and then a sensitive intelligent thoughtful person feels very mournful about his country and, deciding with Brillat-Savarin that "The destiny of nations depends upon what and how they eat," he begins to question.

Why, he asks, are we so ungastronomic as a nation?

Why do we permit and even condone the feeble packaged bread that our men try to keep strong on! [And women . . . and, worst of all, *children*!]

Why do we let our millers rob the wheat of all its goodness, and then buy the wheat germ for one thousand times its value from our druggists so that our children may be strong and healthy?

Why do we go on eating cakes and puddings after good meals, because we always did when we were children?

Why do we talk longingly of the honest beef stew our Aunt Matilda used to make while we spend a dollar or two eating third-rate steamed chicken dipped in batter and fried in a shameful pot of synthetic grease in some roadside hashery?

It is because we are sentimental, probably, and loyal to what we want to remain sweet memories of our younger years. It is because we are proud, and vain, and unwilling to admit our own weaknesses. And most of all it is because we, and almost all American Anglo-Saxon children of the second generation, have been taught when we were young not to mention food or enjoy it publicly.

If we have liked a meringue, or an artful little curl of pastry on a kidney pie, or a toasted walnut placed as only a child would like it right in the middle of a chocolate blancmange, we have not been allowed to cry out with pleasure but instead have been pressed down, frowned at, weighted with a heavy adult reasoning that such display was unseemly, and vulgar, and almost "foreign."

Once when young Walter Scott, who later wrote so many exciting books, was exceptionally hungry and said happily, "*Oh*, what a fine soup! Is it not a *fine* soup, dear Papa?," his father immediately poured a pint of cold water into what was already a pretty thin broth, if the usual family menu was any sample. Mr. Scott did it, he said, to drown the devil.

For too many nice ordinary little Americans the devil has been drowned, so that all their lives afterwards they eat what is set before them, without thought, without comment, and, worst of all, without interest. The result is that our cuisine is often expensively repetitive: we eat what and how and when our parents ate, without thought of natural hungers.

It is not enough to make a child hungry; if he is moderately healthy he will have all the requisites of a normal pig or puppy or plant-aphis, and will eat when he is allowed to, without thought. The important thing, to make him not a pig or puppy, nor even a delicate green insect, is to let him eat from the beginning with thought.

Let him choose his foods, not for what he likes as such, but for what goes with something else, in taste and in texture and in general gastronomic excitement. It is not wicked sensuality, as Walter Scott's father would have thought, for a little boy to prefer buttered toast with spinach for supper and a cinnamon bun with milk for lunch. It is the beginning of a sensitive and thoughtful system of deliberate choice, which as he grows will grow too, so that increasingly he will be able to choose for himself and to weigh values, not only sensual but spiritual.

He will remember, some time when he is a man, that once he decided not to eat a chocolate bar, but to let the taste of a stolen apple ride an hour or two longer on his appreciative tongue. And whatever decision he must make as a man will probably be the solider for that apple he ate so long since.

The ability to choose what food you must eat, and knowingly, will make you able to choose other less transitory things with courage and finesse. A child should be encouraged, not discouraged as so many are, to look at what he eats, and think about it: the juxtapositions of color and flavor and texture . . . and indirectly the reasons why he is eating it and the results it will have on him, if he is an introspective widgin. (If not, the fact that what he eats is not only good but pretty will do him no harm.)

If, with the wolf at the door, there is not very much to eat, the child should know it, but not oppressively. Rather, he should be encouraged to savor every possible bite with one eye on its agreeable nourishment and the other on its fleeting but valuable esthetic meaning, so that twenty years later, maybe, he can think with comfortable delight of the little brown toasted piece of bread he ate with you once in 1942, just before that apartment was closed, and you went away to camp.

It was a nice piece of toast, with butter on it. You sat in the sun under the pantry window, and the little boy gave you a bite, and for both of you the smell of nasturtiums warming in the April air would be mixed forever with the savor between your teeth of melted butter and toasted bread, and the knowledge that although there might not be any more, you had shared that piece with full consciousness on both sides, instead of a shy awkward pretense of not being hungry.

[I feel, even more strongly than I did in 1942, that one of the most important things about a child's gastronomical present, in relation to his future, gastronomical and otherwise, is a good *respect* for food. It horrifies me to see contemporary mothers numbly cooking and then throwing away uneaten lamb chops, beans, toast; mussed but unsavored puddings; deliberately spilled or bedabbled milk. I think children should be given small portions of food, according to their natures, and allowed to cope with them at their own speeds, but *finish* them, before more is trotted out in the currently fashionable pediatric pattern. . . . They learn their capacities. They learn good manners. Above all, they learn to respect the food so many other children cry for.]

All men are hungry. They always have been. They must eat, and when they deny themselves the pleasures of carrying out that need, they are cutting off part of their possible fullness, their natural realization of life, whether they are poor or rich.

It is a sinful waste of human thought and energy and deep delight, to teach little children to pretend that they should not care or mention what they eat. How sad for them when they are men! Then they may have to fight, or love, or make other children, and they won't know how to do it fully, with satisfaction, completely, because when they were babies they wanted to say, "*Oh*, what a fine soup!" and instead only dared murmur, "More, please, Papa!"

How to
Lure the Wolf

She wrenched from her brow a diamond and eyed it with
contempt, took from her pocket a sausage and contemplated
it with respect and affection.

Peg Woffington, CHARLES READE

Let us sing the praises, willy-nilly, of the wolf in human form
or otherwise who can with straight face and unwrinkled muzzle
woo a tousled kitchen maid. His muzzle, wrinkled or smooth,
must be insensate, thus to ignore her locks all heavy with the
perfumes of the frying pan. His so-called face, straight or wolf-
ishly crooked, must either be without eyes or unduly charita-
ble, thus to forgo at least one cruel glance at her shiny nose and
her gnawed lips and the chapped remnants of her last-week's
manicure.

In other words, any normal wolf would be a fool to take a
tousled kitchen maid at her own face value, since the very fact
that she is tousled should prove to him her sluttish nature.

If you want to lure a wolf, no matter what his form, there are
certain tricks known heretofore among a chosen few, which can
at last be released to the general class of kitchen maids (the plural

of which was long held to be *kitchen midden* by one otherwise erudite scholar. He may have been the same one, although it seems somewhat improbable, who wrote an essay in his younger days about the pleasures of picking dewberries in the Maine woods in the summertime. It was not until his form-master was removed from the classroom in a state of near hysteria that this future semanticist learned that dewberries are what rabbits make as well as what they nibble).

One way to look your prettiest in the kitchen, and make the wolf think that even if his hot breath whuffs through the keyhole and ruffles your very curls you are nigh adamant, is to put up a little mirror.

Myself, I have a right nice mahogany frame that once held a prim silhouette, with a band of spotted dingy gold inside it. The mirror within is wavy and cheap, and the whole thing hangs on a wall that shakes and sends it all crooked every time anyone bangs a door in the house, and I have to lean over the vegetable bin and squint like sixty to see anything at all, but probably I give myself a reassuring look or tweak or pat by way of that mirror at least five times a day, and feel the better for it.

Sometimes I look into it confidently, hot and steamy from stirring a sauce, but feeling quite attractive, when somebody pulls at the front-door bell, and I stop short and say, "Hey!" There is not much to do about it then. I have struck bottom. But usually I look into it when the bell peals, and I can see either that things are under control beautifully or that a certain amount of smoothing, poking, and composing will do some good.

And even if nobody else notices, the fact that I have seen my own disorder and recognized it makes a great psychological difference. I have always felt that if the Prince of Wales or Charles Boyer came to the door, I would much rather know about the smudge on my nose than not. [Today I am not so sure.]

Sometimes, especially in small apartments, dinner guests arrive at one door before you can snake through another to dull the finish on your nose and get back before the peas turn black. So a little shelf under the mirror ought to be very nice indeed. On it you could put a compact, and a lipstick perhaps. Neither should have a strong perfume, since any fabricated odor mixed with the heady and if possible agreeable smells of the meal-in-progress would be more than unpleasant.

Some women keep a bottle of hand lotion in the cupboard. (Horrible thought for blackouts, when they may reach for the salad oil or the vinegar!) If you use such a lotion anyway at other times this is probably all right. You must be careful, though, never to put it religiously and righteously on your hands, as the advertisements tell you to, and then pull apart the leaves for a salad or peel tomatoes or some such thing: the result will be nauseous.

Instead, you may quite economically do what I have done for a great many years, and use whatever sweet-smelling oil or fat or grease is wandering around begging for a taker. If you unwrap a quarter-pound of butter, rub the paper on your hands before you throw it away. If you are making salad dressing, catch the last drop of oil from the bottle on your fingers. If you mix ground meat with tomato juice and egg and crumbs for some kind of loaf, rub the film of fat into your hands instead of washing it off at once; it will soon vanish, and you will have smoother fingers and more firmly beautiful nails.

Rubber gloves are supposed to be a good idea, and indeed rare and strange wonders are worked in spite of them in surgeries, where living rather than dead flesh is carved to make more life. In kitchens I think it is perhaps better to be unprotected: few chefs have hands as valuable as a good doctor's, or as well trained, and the common tasks need not be so difficult as to do harm to hypersensitive fingers. [I know more now. I even know a fine chef who is diabetic, and must wear gloves on his very dry hands because of the insulin he absorbs, and the way his skin would disappear if he did not . . . or so he explains it.]

It is true that onions or garlic often leave a wretched haunting stink, and one not yet associated in the common male mind with glamor. The answer to that is to slice any of the bulbs (onions, scallions, garlic, leeks, chives) under running water. Then, as soon as the job is done, wash the knife and your hands thoroughly in cold and still running water, and *then*, if you are a fussbudget, rub a cut lemon on them. And then again, if by chance your skin is the kind that holds such undignified odors, simply stop slicing onions and all their ilk.

Washing dishes, according to advertisements and a large percentage of the radio dramas, has ruined many an otherwise lovely woman's chance for happiness. Her hands, rough, chapped, utterly repellent, have driven Mr. Right away. Then, if she has been wise, or perhaps even had a neighbor who tipped her off in time, she has given herself a ten-day test and washed in ordinary soap with her left hand and in super-oxygenized Drift-O with her right hand, in a miraculous test of legerdemain.

In seven or eight days she has seen the difference: her roughened, reddened left hand has shamed her. In another week, or even less, that hand, all white and silken, sparkles with a great big glorious solitaire, and burns with the hidden ecstasy of Mr. Right's first and perhaps last kiss. All is well, and from that day forward she washes dishes with just oodles of soapsy sudsy bubble-squubble Drift-O.

Or, Mr. Right or no Mr. Right, she never uses soap at all. It is surprising how clean dishes can be, and how effortless the task can be, and how small the soap bill can be, given a small stream of moderately hot water and a stiff brush. With a certain amount of practice your hands, even the one holding the plate or cup, need never be in the water . . . and if you scrape the plates first, which of course you would do, the sink stays clean, the drains stay fresh, and your brush, which you get free from the Fuller man, lasts for a boringly long time.

You hold the plate under the running water, turn it with one hand and scrub it with the other, and put it in a rack on the drainboard. When you have collected a few, you dry them—before they are cold.

This scheme sounds rather dreamy, put down in cold print, but it works well, much to the disgust of better and older dishwashers than I could ever be.

Or do I mean that? They may be *older* . . . but I would be willing to bet fifty thousand Chincoteagues that never in my life have I put a dish with a slippery bottom into a china cupboard, and that not one of them could say the same. Of course there is no proof of my wager, except my own conscience. That, on the subject of clean dishes at least, is clear as an autumn sky. I have taxed the soul of many an experienced housekeeper because I have refused to make a great pan of suds and douse glasses and dishes in it . . . and with utter smugness I still feel that I use no more water, and certainly a lot less soap, and that I bother the skin of my hands not at all, by my slipshod easy method of scraping dishes and then scrubbing them under a little hot water. [I continue to get letters of disgusted protest about this system. I continue not only to believe in it but to practice it, and I begin to suspect that I probably have consistently cleaner dishes than any other "general housekeeper" I have ever met. Such bland self-satisfaction merits, and generously *gets* a dressing down.]

Naturally this method presupposes at least a limited supply of that. In case of shortages or broken water lines or some such wartime inconvenience, other means would be found by any ingenious woman. Probably the easiest, and one perhaps enforced whether or no, would be to stop eating at all.

In case you are fortunate enough to have a kitchen with a stove in it and something to cook on it when you read this, you may also have a dish that calls for, say, one onion browned in two tablespoonfuls of fat. You may also have pretty brown or gold or black hair hanging in loose curls about your face, or even skinned up into a modish if unbecoming nob on top of your head [. . . or, nowadays, snipped as short as Peter Pan's].

In any case you should tie a washable scarf about what hairs you have when you fry onions or broil a steak or whip together a mixed-grill for your monthly treat. You will be much more alluring afterwards, even unto the next day, for fumes from fine dishes have a marked tendency to linger in the mind's covering as well as the mind.

Indeed, it can be said that fumes linger, period. They lurk in cupboards. They drift subtly through closed doors, no matter what cunning draft you may enforce, at risk of double pneumonia, through the kitchenette. They hang in the curtains, and fall out at you two nights later like overripe shreds of dead ghost.

There is not much to do about it; you either like fried onion or hot cabbage salad enough to endure them, or you eat lettuce or green peas instead.

Or you compromise by covering one fume with another. [Jeanne Bonamour believed firmly that a couple of cloves of garlic boiled with cabbage or cauliflower would hold down the distasteful fumes. What she did was double them! But her cauliflower was the best I ever ate.]

You can do it, according to the Stark Realism school, by lighting a crumbled piece of newspaper and dashing through the rooms with it. You can, much more effectively [. . . and tidily . . .] pour a drop or two of oil of eucalyptus or pine on a hot shovel and wave it around. If you want to feel like a character from one of the James brothers' looser romantic moments you can float a few drops of oil of lavender in a silver bowl filled with hot water.

And if you are somebody I do not know and furthermore do not care if I ever meet, you can burn a little cone of incense. [Various kinds of liquid candles like Air-Wick have come into our lives since this was written. They evaporate much as any candle burns, and they are based, or so I surmise, on extracts of live chlorophyll. I like them, as a last but reliable resort. Better are strong plants of philodendron, preferably grown around porous slabs of moistened bark. In the face of possible horror from hidebound nannies, I say they are wonderful in nurseries, to wash and sweeten the sometimes overburdened air.]

Or you can broil the meat, fry the onions, stew the garlic in the red wine . . . and ask me to supper. I'll not care, really, even if your nose is a little shiny, so long as you are self-possessed and sure that wolf or no wolf, your mind is your own and your heart is another's and therefore in the right place.

How to Drink
to the Wolf

They eat, they drink, and in communion sweet
Quaff immortality and joy.

JOHN MILTON

One infallible way to know that a country is at war is to read of
the increased activity of the militant prohibitionists. Another
fairly good way is to read statistics about the rise in pub-
crawling, or as some people call it, alcoholic consumption.
Which comes first, the chicken or the egg . . . the blue-nose or
the red-nose?

Whichever, there can be no doubt that war's fever breeds
drought as well as thirst, and that for countless centuries some
men have frowned and scolded and some men have drunk
deeper as Mars squeezed them.

Less than a month after our country entered this last war,
Washington prohibitionists were praying and proving that
Pearl Harbor, not to mention France's Fall, was directly trace-
able to the bottle. At the same time other men in Washington
(not to mention Pearl Harbor and perhaps even Fallen France's

safe cellars) were wetting their throats and drinking to what they hoped was their own and the nation's health.

If you happen to be unencumbered by childhood's scruples and maturity's sage ponderings, you will have gone to a great many cocktail parties in your time and will have decided, along with almost every other thing human left alive, that they are anathema. They are expensive. They are dull. They are good for a time, like a dry Martini, and like that all-demanding drink they can lift you high and then drop you hideously into a slough of boredom, morbidity, and indigestion.

When you reach this point of perception, and admit once for all that such routs shall see no more of you, there is but one step more. Then you will decide that from now on you'll drink as you please, and with whom, and where, and how . . . and what.

Given a number of present-day ways to be poor (and whether you earn an immediately impressive salary or not, you will feel poor for several days or hours before each new check is cashed, in wartime), there is one sure way to feel poorer. That is to form the specious habit of stopping at the local grogshop, the Greek's around the corner, Ye Cozie Nooke Cocktail Lounge. Even if cocktails keep their prewar prices, the liquor is bound to fluctuate in quality, and it is easy as scat to pile up astonishing bills in one or two predinner drop-ins, and even more horrendous hangovers.

The first thing to do, of course, is to stop going there. The next thing is to find a reputable substitute, since even a young man cannot too easily quit such solace as is offered by the dim jukey confines of the neighborhood gin mill.

One of the best antidotes, if anything so pleasant could be termed so damningly, is to decide the person you like best to drink with and see if you can arrange to have a predinner nip with her or him . . . alone. *Alone* does not necessarily connotate *salaciously*, *lasciviously*, or even amorously, since if you like a person well enough to drink alone with him, he will be the kind who will have worked all day and be as glad as you to sit back and absorb a little quick relaxation from a glass and then eat, quaffing immortality and joy. He will if possible be your husband or your own true love, and you will find in this sudden quiet and peacefulness something that has sometimes seemed much too far from you both, lately. [I consider myself more fortunate than most women in that I know several good drinking companions of my own sex. They are for the most part well past sixty, a significant fact in the study of Alcohol in Modern Society, I imagine. . . . The best of them, eighty-two last Christmas, has taught me much of both self-control and sensual pleasure from her enjoyment of a weekly glass of dry champagne.]

If you (and occasionally Z and A, but never everyone in between) are used to hard liquor, you would do well to stick to it, for a time at least. In comparison with bar prices, it costs very little to buy an ordinary but reputable gin by the gallon jug. [There are few such jugs, but in spite of local laws most good liquor stores will still give discounts on case-lots of fifths or quarts.] Dry vermouth from California or New York or South America are equally reputable and not at all ordinary. These two mixed knowingly with a little ice make a mighty passable martini by any standards, and are doubly titillating drunk for a change in the airy sanctum of your own or a good friend's room.

Whiskey drinkers, whose name (to coin a phrase again) is legion, will drink Scotch, or bourbon, or rye, *or* blended spirits. They rarely admit being able to swallow more than one of the varieties. If you are in this general group, either swear off or choose a brew you can afford, and then save enough money until you can buy a case of it. (All this, granted that you are a moderate drinker-for-pleasure, and not a thirsty unhappy soul who must empty every bottle willy-nilly to drown some worm in the brain.)

Liquor by the case is generally about 10 percent less expensive than by the bottle, and generally it disappears at least 10 percent faster, so you must gauge your own purse and proclivities. If you can accept a case loose in the pantry with equanimity, use it sparingly but well, on yourself and your favorite friends.

Have a good drink before dinner, in comparative peace. Try drinking about one part whiskey to two of plain water, without ice. Old-time drinkers swear that is the only way to treat a good liquor, and after the first shock, when your palate expected a cold watered mouthful, you will probably agree. It is a better drink, and it will make a surprising difference not only in your digestion but your budget. Both will be stronger for the lack of ice and synthetic bubbles.

If you are even more haunted by the wolf at the door and still like your toddy, cut yourself down with some brutality to the starkness of sherry [. . . or a good vermouth]. At first it will seem pale, innocuous, a child's tipple. After a week you will look forward to it, and if you are sensible and fortunate enough to have fallen on a decent if much-maligned California bottle, you will tot up your budget with some relief.

Sherry by the bottle, naturally, costs more than sherry by the gallon. Sherry by the gallon, in the Eastern states at least, is often shameful. Try to find a good merchant. . . Italians usually have a nice feeling for the fortified wines . . . and if you can trust him at all you can trust him not to give you a jug half-full of chemicals. Then decant it yourself; you can buy a ten-cent funnel and use the washed vermouth bottles from your occasional martinis. A gallon will last a long time and should cost up or down around a dollar, in spite of what the self-styled connoisseurs will say. [I cannot believe this was true, even an eon of nine years ago! Surely I meant "quart," not "gallon" . . . and I still do.]

An agreeable drink with a surprising lift to it is the following:

Half-and-Half Cocktail

½ *cup dry vermouth*	*ice*
½ *cup dry sherry*	*dash of angostura bitters if*
½ *lemon*	*desired*

Pour vermouth and sherry into shaker over cracked ice. Add lemon juice and bitters. Stir well, pour into glasses and top with the rest of the lemon rind.

Little salty crackers or a bowl of freshly toasted nuts are good with sherry, or with Half-and-Half. These drinks can be served in the old martini glasses, and afterwards you can have a china pitcher or a carafe of wine on the table.

If your sherry merchant is honest about the sherry he will probably be honest about other wines as well, and you should with impunity be able to fill a gallon jug for little more than a dollar with good characterful red or white wine, not notable but not infamous. [This is possible only if you know the vintner and can go to his cellar, jug in hand. But there are several reputable blended table wines available now, for about three dollars a gallon. They make an occasional ceremonial bottle of fine wine taste even finer.] It should be the kind that makes good food taste better, and leaves a nice clean budding on your tongue, and makes the next morning seem fortunate rather than a catastrophe.

It is surprising how many confirmed likkadrinkas blossom and unwind and emerge from their professionally hard shells on such a liquid accompaniment to a good supper. Some insist later that it is the shock to their system . . . the sudden shift from grain to grape . . . that has caused the change. Most of them, any subtle host can see, are secretly or unconsciously relieved not to have to lap up their usual quota of premeal highballs or cocktails.

A pleasant aperitif, as well as a good chaser for a short quick whiskey, as well again for a fine supper drink, is beer . . . if you like it. Beer in big cities can be sent out for in a bucket to the corner pub, even from Park Avenue, but probably even on Park Avenues, in New York or elsewhere, it is better in bottles.

It should be bought by the case, because it is cheaper that way and easier to have delivered. You should save the tops. (I cannot think just why, but I am sure that something is done with them. The beer-man would know.) And of course you should save the bottles, instead of doing several other obvious things with them.

The present war will probably affect such fantastic problems as the one involving the transportation of lager from Milwaukee to Sunset Beach, California, and in the main it may be a good thing.

There are a thousand small honest breweries in this country that because they have been too poor and localized to compete with the big boys have been forced to close, or else operate under famous names while they turned out yeast, or hops, or some other important but unnamed ingredient of the main company's beer. Now, with trains full of soldiers and supplies rather than pale ale, perhaps people far from the great breweries will turn again to their local beer factories and discover, as their fathers did thirty years ago, that a beer carried quietly three miles is better than one shot across three thousand on a fast freight. [I am sorry that this did not happen. War seemingly made it easier and cheaper than ever to drink Milwaukee beer in Sunset Beach.]

Beer is a good drink. ("Teetotalers seem to die the same as others," A. P. Herbert wrote once between sessions in the House of Commons. "So what's the use of knocking off the beer?") Wine is a good drink, if you can get it, and now as never before in this country you can get it with confidence that it will be honest and full-bodied and all the other things that even grudging tasters say about a decent drink of it.

Hard liquors like gin and whiskey are more difficult to get, especially if you are thinking of economy, but they can still be found (circa 1942). [As I remember, the worst result of a World War II block was a flood of Argentine gin. Sensitive martini-boys and Gibson-girls still shudder. . . . They took to tequila and vodka, but only in desperation and fortunately for only a few weeks.] If you cannot afford them (and will admit it, which is rare), you might try to find an honest but unscrupulous druggist and buy a quart of good alcohol. Then, armed with this recipe, which stems via a Junior Leaguer from Ohio through Tiflis in what was once known as Georgia (Europe), you can make a mighty powerful drink that will treat you honestly and please you meanwhile.

A Vodka

[*This is still a good recipe, and worthy of individual study and experimentation. My uncle Walter, the most accomplished early-morning drinker I have ever known, says it is superlative in tomato juice.*]

1 *quart water*	½ *orange rind, shaved*
1 *teaspoon glycerin or sugar*	1 *quart alcohol*
1 *lemon rind, shaved*	

Simmer first 4 ingredients very gently about 20 minutes. Remove from stove. Add alcohol and cover instantly with a tight lid. Let cool and strain.

To make a very acceptable liqueur add more fruit shavings and a spoonful or so of honey.

A Mr. Furnas, who writes more wisely and less pompously than most men about other men, bread, and destiny in a book called *Man, Bread and Destiny*, discusses at some length the various prescriptions throughout the ages for love potions. He mentions all the known ones, like Spanish fly and pork-chops-with-pepper, and a great many less prevalent charms. Finally he decides, and almost with a sigh of relief, that probably the best excitant in the world is sweet music and a moderate amount of alcohol! [Just lately I heard a modern lover state his vision of pure bliss, unconscious of his parody of Omar Khayyam: "A horn of gin, a good cigar, and *you*, Babe."]

When he writes so sensibly, it is hard not to say, along with the governor of South Carolina who was talking to the governor of North Carolina, that it's a long time between drinks, especially when there is sweet music and your love and good liquor. Then you can raise a glass to the wolf with impunity and a courage that is real, no matter how alcoholic, and know that even if you regret it tomorrow, you have been a man without qualms either amorous or budgetary tonight. [I believe, even more strongly now than then, that the important thing about drinking is that it be done for *pleasure*. Then, and then only, the sad fear of alcoholism never rises from its slough to haunt us, and neither our manners nor our digestions can be criticized.]

How Not to
Be an Earthworm

Streamlined to the ultimate for functional performance the
earthworm blindly eats his way, riddling and honeycombing
the ground to a depth of ten feet or more as he swallows.
Anatomy Underfoot, J.-J. CONDE

[This whole chapter has the faintly phosphorescent humor of
decay about it. It is as outmoded as a treatise on how to treat
javelin-wounds, now that we know even earthworms are not
inviolate.]

Other wars have made men live like rats, or wolves, or lice,
but until this one, except perhaps for the rehearsal in Spain, we
have never lived like earthworms.

Now we bend our minds, with the surprised intensity of any
nonplused [In the face of continued disapproval I think this
should have two esses, just as I think the word busses is proper
in the plural for both a vehicle and a kiss. Buses, indeed! I am *not*
nonplused.] creatures, to existing as gracefully as possible without many of the things we have always accepted as our due:
light, free air, fresh foods, prepared according to our tastes. It

can be done, of course, since we are humans as well as rats, wolves, lice, and earthworms.

You may have heard of one woman in England who withdrew to her tidy little bomb-shelter in the garden when the first siren sounded, and emerged, rather dreamily, some two weeks later. She'd been quite comfy, she told her worried neighbors, but she did hope the blinkin' raids would not always last quite so long.

There is more than a modicum of British deadpan humor in this wry story, as you will agree if you have ever stood, even for a few minutes, in one of the dreadful little strongboxes we are meant to hide in when bombs fall. No matter how much effort architects and decorators spend on making them habitable, they are shameful places, cramped and stuffy and ugly. They are a means to an end, which is to survive, but they have only that virtue.

Blacked-out rooms are another thing. Usually they are places we recognize, with familiar chairs and pictures. They are not cells or holes to hide in, but chambers with their lights blinded from the outside, where we can continue in an almost normal way our nightly life of supper, and reading, and playing the phonograph or rummy and always the game of Being Casual.

Blackouts happen at night, of course, and so, usually does dinner. For that reason it is wise, if possible, to have the kitchen one of the rooms most adequately equipped to operate normally under the various restrictions of your neighborhood and your own common sense, when the siren sounds.

In a small house you can make this one room into a very pleasant place for the whole family . . . unless you are unfortunate enough to have what used to be called a "kitchenette," which means that it is impossibly small, even for its original function. In that case, you should try to black out both it and the next room, never forgetting that there are a few other functions as necessary, if not as pleasant, as eating, and that an easily accessible toilet is more important than any stove.

Since this country went to war, a great deal has been done to prepare us for emergencies (a polite word for bombings, invasions, and many other ugly things). Much has been good, and intelligent, and it is too easy and perhaps very wrong to criticize some of the less good and intelligent moves. It is hard not to wonder, however, how some of the sensible women who are planning such things as emergency rations can be so blandly impractical, especially when most of them are graduate home economists and dieticians.

There are many lists being prepared by various organizations, mapping out twenty-four-hour emergency rations for school children, hospitals, and so forth. Here is a sample [I refer to this later as "nauseating," but no one word is strong enough to suggest my scorn of it, esthetically as well as biochemically. It is a shocking example of gastronomical panic, and if it were heeded would soon reduce us to malnourished as well as spiritually weakened creatures, past much harm from bursting atoms.] that is of course made up of foods that can be stored indefinitely, and which have been calculated down to the last soda cracker for five hundred people:

BREAKFAST
Tomato juice
Peanut butter
Soda crackers or Melba toast
Hot milk chocolate

DINNER
Spaghetti with tomato puree
Corned beef

Peas and carrots
Soda crackers
Penny chocolate bars

SUPPER OR LUNCHEON
Tomato soup with canned milk
Soda crackers
Fruit cup
Graham crackers

These three meals, to be prepared for such a large number of people, most of whom are supposed to be children, would be heated on "a barbecue or make-shift inside camp cooking equipment," the folder says!

Aside from the obvious fact that few people eat three hot meals a day, even in peacetime ("Warm foods are not the only 'warming foods.' . . . Get out of the habit of cooking a hot meal every day," the British Ministry of Food urges in one of its regular newspaper bulletins.), it is foolish to think of the number of plates and cups and utensils that would have to be washed to provide for these impractical and nauseating feasts.

Have the earnest ladies of the Parent-Teachers Advisory Board forgotten that water may be as much of a problem as fuel, if things are so upset that five hundred people are hiding together in the basement of a schoolhouse? The old economy of paper cups and plates exists no longer, and the idea of washing at least twenty-five hundred different vessels into a passably sterile state is an uncomfortable one.

There are other problems than the main one of serving this pathetic attempt at a "balanced diet" to five hundred ill-assorted and bewildered people. The dieticians must begin, always with the hope that it will never be needed, to borrow knowledge from the women in England, who after the countless nights of this war have gradually evolved their own rules.

In the meantime, you feel, as almost all people do without even realizing it, that you would rather be at home than anywhere else, if enemy planes are scouting somewhere in the air. As long as it can be done without too much danger, that is just where you should be, and aside from the inescapable unpleasantness of your reasons for being there, it can be downright entertaining to spend your evenings in your blacked-out rooms.

There is something innately desirable about a room shut off completely from the eyes of other humans. [I continue to agree with something Colette once wrote about the primitive satisfaction of a low dark place to eat in. This is a fine conversational gambit . . . who can resist discoursing on *his* ideas of the perfect dining room, whether he be dyspeptic, ascetic, or simply hungry?] It makes you feel protected, probably the way a kitten feels when it hides in a coat-sleeve, or a child under the blankets. Unfortunately, like the coat-sleeve or the blankets, it can be very stuffy, as the English have discovered. Intelligent designers are thinking and writing about that, and such magazines as the January 1942, *Architectural Forum* are very helpful.

Given a moderately well-ventilated kitchen, which is large enough in itself or is next to another blacked-out room, you can live there with people you like and find life decent indeed.

The people in England have found that electricity usually stays on longer than gas in an actual bombing, so most well-equipped private shelters have little electric grills in them, or at least toasters and hot plates. Now would be a good time to get out the old chafing dish, if you have not already done it. (The next thing is to hope that you can buy alcohol for it, but sufficient unto the day is the evil of that particular shortage.) [Ordinary rubbing compounds will do, in spite of their weird smells and the ugly incrustations they make upon the copper.]

In spite of your optimistic refusal to believe that anything could happen to *your* gas main or *your* power lines, it is a wise thing, if you know that you are to be blacked out that night, to cook as much food as you can during the day. Make things that can be reheated or served cold.

Another good reason for cooking while it is light is that few kitchens are as well ventilated as they should be at the best of times, so that at night with the windows closed and several people in the room, the air should not be overheated and filled with steams and fumes of food. This is especially true if you are reduced to cooking with an open flame or with coal oil: the air quickly becomes poor.

It is better, for the same reason, to cook things that do not have too strong a smell. Cabbage, for instance, is unwise. Kidneys, unless they are prepared beforehand, are too strong in the air. (They are easy, though, to fix in a chafing dish, smell or no smell.)

In the old days, before Stuka and blitz became a part of even childish chitchat, every practical guide to cookery urged you to keep a well-filled emergency shelf in your kitchen or pantry. Emergency is another word that has changed its inner shape; when Marion Harland and Fanny Farmer used it they meant unexpected guests. You may, too, in an ironical way, but you hope to God they are the kind who will never come.

It is often a delicate point, now, to decide when common sense ends and hoarding begins. Preparing a small stock of practical boxed and canned goods for a blackout shelf, in direct relation to the size of your family, is quite another thing from buying large quantities of bottled shrimps and canape wafers and meat pastes, or even unjustified amounts of more sensible foods.

Probably the best way to stock your shelf is to buy two cans of vegetables and so forth when you need only one, if your local rationing allows it. Make a list of what you would like to have, and gradually accumulate it, if you can afford to.

Even if you cannot afford to, try to put aside at least an Iron ration of a few cans of tomato juice, a box of cube sugar (to eat for warmth and quick energy), a little tea, a sealed box of whole-wheat wafers, some tinned beef.

When you buy in cans, remember that many of the prepared "luncheon loaves" are extremely salty. It is impractical to give your family such food in blackouts, especially if the toilet is far away or nonexistent and the drinking water is limited.

A useful thing to have on your shelf is a supply of ginger-snaps or vanilla wafers. [Much as I hate to admit it, weary English housewives have convinced me that packaged puddings are heaven-sent for such cookery: they have enough sugar in them to bolster energy, and even made with water they are palatable, at least to hungry and uneasy children and the gaffers.] These innocuous (or obnoxious, if you feel that way about them) cookies are useful at turning a can of fruit into a somewhat more nourishing and much more attractive dish, if you can put them all together and broil them for a few minutes, with the fruit on top. A little butter and brown sugar and even a dash of sherry will help.

Vanilla wafers may bring tears of anguish to the eyes of some self-respecting gourmets, but canned beef-gravy will make them sob aloud. And yet . . . may I be forgiven for admitting it . . . or may I? . . . canned beef-gravy is a "natural" for you if you have someone in your family who feels faint and weak unless he smells at least synthetic meat once a day. You can make many a good tricked dish, with a few mushrooms, some leftover rice, and a dash of wine, if you have one of those frightening, efficient cans of "rich brown *meat* gravy" on hand. It is spurious, maybe. It is chicanery. But it is economical and useful psychologically, especially if you are three miles from a market and the siren blows just as you are pumping up your bike-tire.

Another useful thing of doubtful origin for your blackout

shelf is a moderate supply of cheeses in glass. The damnable things are fakes; they admit it on the labels . . . *simulated* Romano, Cheddar *type*, and so on. They are flatulently proud of being pasteurized. But they perform a special function, I think, in making people feel hungry. [I deplore the stupid overuse of monosodium glutamate, but in various "flavoring salts," called anything from Tang-oh to Mete-dee-lite, it does manage to lend a valuable if fleeting desirability to basically dull dishes.]

Cheese has always been a food that both sophisticated and simple humans love. And even if some doctors may not feel that it is wise to eat it, in a time of peril and unspoken fear it is an anesthetic and can make your guests, your own self, feel slightly stimulated by its unmistakable flavor and more than a little reassured to know that it still exists. Put a little bit on crackers, or on crisp toast if your oven is still working. Try it on a tired factory worker some day, or a nervous neighbor, with a glass of milk if possible or a cup of tea, and watch the unfolding of a lot of spiritual tendrils that were drawn up into a tight heedless tangle. [The lunch of draymen and farmers-at-market in French Switzerland is one of the best in the world: a slab of bread, a cut of slightly grainy mountain-cheese, a glass of thin white wine . . . I have seen it work miracles of restoration.]

If you are used to drinking, and can, it is pleasant to have whiskey or a good stable wine in your cupboard. A glass in your hand makes the ominous sky seem very high above you.

If by chance you want to be out in the streets, benefit by many a Londoner's experience and carry a little flask, since welcoming pubs are few and far between, and none too eager to open their doors even to old friends when unidentified planes are reported within sound of the listening posts.

(Do you remember that bar in Berne, during the Munich business, the night before what we all thought would be M-Day? There was a total blackout, and you went down a long hall through patent-leather curtains and then sat with a lot of other silent people in the dim room, while the tropical birds in the glass walls, which were really cages that imprisoned you caught in another and still another cage, flitted and screamed silently behind the glass. Everybody sat with a waiting look. It would have been better to stay away, probably.)

It is practical for blackouts, as well as for general "common sense in the kitchen" to cook more than you need for one meal. There are many simple recipes that can be made into a whole meal if you have some boiled rice handy, or some leftover green peas, or a bowl of cold cooked meat or spaghetti or almost anything you can think of (except maybe fried oysters!).

If you and your household are in a state of active emergency, you will survive, probably, without heat or light or anything but what you can scrape from the shelves. This picture is not one you care to dwell on, but it is a possibility. If it comes to that, no book on earth can help you, but only your inborn sense of caution and balance and protection: the same thing cats feel sometimes, or birds or elephants. Everything resolves itself into a feeling that you will survive if you are meant to survive, and every cell in your body believes that.

If you are not in a state of emergency, but merely living as so many people have lived for many months now, taking sirens in your stride and ration cards with a small cautious grin, you will be able to make very good meals indeed for the people who live with you. As long as the gas or the electric current supply you, your stove will function and your kitchen will be warm and savory. Use as many fresh things as you can, always, and then trust to luck and your blackout cupboard and what you have decided, inside yourself, about the dignity of man.

How to
Practice True Economy

Mere parsimony is not economy. . . . Expense, and great
expense, may be an essential part of true economy.
Letters to a Noble Lord, EDMUND BURKE, 1796

There is supposed to be something intrinsically satisfying
about writing the last chapter of a book, even if it is written before the end. There should be something doubly so about writing of half-forgotten luxuries and half-remembered delicate
impossible dishes at the end of a book of resolutely practical recipes for foxing the wolf and keeping him either at his proper dis-
tance, or well-jointed in a stewpan. It should be like waking
from a dream of your loved one, and finding perfume on your
lips.

Such impossible delights are necessary, now and then, to
your soul, and your body, too. You can cope with economy for
only so long. ("So long" is one of those ambiguous phrases. It
means "so long as you do not feel sick at the sight of a pocketbook.")

When you think you can stand no more of the wolf's snuffing
under the door and keening softly on cold nights, throw discre-

tion into the laundry bag, put candles on the table, and for your own good if not the pleasure of an admiring audience make one or another of the recipes in this chapter. And buy yourself a bottle of wine, or make a few cocktails, or have a long open-hearted discussion of cheeses with the man on the corner who is an alien but still loyal if bewildered.

It is plain that a great many of the things in the following recipes are impossible to find, now. That immediately puts the whole chapter in the same class as Samarkand and Xanadu and the *terrasse* of the Café de la Paix. It is perhaps just as well; for a time there are other things than anchovies that must be far from actuality.

Sit back in your chair, then. Drop a few years from your troubled mind. Let the cupboard of your thoughts fill itself with a hundred ghosts that long ago, in 1939, used to be easy to buy and easy to forget. [This therapy, unconscious or deliberate, is known to any prisoner of war or woe, and some of the world's most delectable cookbooks have been written, at least conversationally and now and then actually, in concentration camps and cell-blocks.] Permit your disciplined inner self to relax, and think of caviar, and thick cream, and fat little pullets trotting through an oak grove rich with truffles, "musky, fiery, savory, mysterious." Close your eyes to the headlines and your ears to sirens and the threatenings of high explosives, and read instead the sweet nostalgic measures of these recipes, impossible yet fond.

Shrimp Pâté

4 *pounds fresh shelled cooked shrimp or 6 cans dry-pack shrimp*	3 *tablespoons lemon juice*
	½ *cup mayonnaise*
1 *onion, minced very fine*	*salt, pepper, dry mustard, whatever other spice you want*
½ *cup melted butter*	

[Now I use a full cup of melted butter, and more if the paste seems dry.]

   Mash the clean shrimp very fine in a big bowl with a potato masher, and add the onion as you do it. When you can mash no more, pour in the melted butter, mixing it thoroughly. Add the lemon juice and mayonnaise, and continue to pound it. It will be a stiff paste. Season it highly: if you plan to use it within two days use fresh herbs at your discretion, but if you will be keeping it in the icebox use powdered condiments.

   Pack the mixture into a mold, and press it down well. Chill it for at least twelve hours in an icebox. When you are ready to serve, turn it out and slice it thin with a sharp hot knife. [I used to eat potted shrimps by the scoopful, in a small swank restaurant in London. They were shelled, whole and tiny, held firmly together in a little fat jar by an aromatic butter. I should think San Francisco's "bay shrimps" would be almost as good for such a forthright accessory to the pleasures of the table . . . but the shrimps must indeed be tiny, no longer than a bee, no thicker than a violet's stem.]

Or leave it in the presentable mold, preferably an oblong one, and serve it slice by slice as the *maîtres d'hôtel* used to do in little places like the Roy Gourmet and big little places like Lipp's and enormous little places like the Ritz, or the Casino at Evian in summer. There are still a few restaurants in the world that can think about *pâtés de maison*, and one of the best of their heady, almost phosphorescent, pastes is made essentially after this recipe—with perhaps a bristol mortar instead of a plain bowl and potato masher, and a good dash of smooth ancient brandy to lace it all together, just before it is packed into the mold.

Such a paste can be kept for weeks or months, or perhaps even for years, if it contains enough spices and alcohol, is correctly sealed into its mold with coagulated fat, and is kept reasonably cold. Given these three prime benefits, it can be produced when you will, like a mad maiden aunt, or a first edition (in Russian, naturally) of *Crime and Punishment*.

Eggs with anchovies. Ah me, to put it mildly! The recipe comes from an American woman who, for various reasons both sociological and esthetic, lived in Switzerland before this war. Although she was almost a stranger to me, I admired her house and many of the meals she served there, high above the lake with the vineyards pressing as close as their Swiss discretion dared against the terrace and the kitchen and the wide windows. She was I . . . and her recipe was good.

Eggs with Anchovies

8	*large fresh eggs*	2	*tablespoons chopped parsley*
2	*tins or 1 cup filet of anchovies*	½	*cup grated Parmesan cheese*
3	*cups rich thick cream*		*fresh-ground pepper*
1	*cup broiled mushrooms (can be tinned) in pieces*		

Mash the filets of anchovies in the bottom of a shallow baking dish (save oil for a salad dressing). Mix the cream with them, and put the dish in a hot oven.

Stir two or three times after it has started to bubble, turning in the golden crust. Add the mushrooms and the parsley.

When reduced about one-third, turn off the oven. Remove the dish, and break the eggs carefully into it. Put the cheese over them, and the pepper. Then put back into the lowest part of the oven, and when the gentle heat has made the eggs firm but not hard, usually in about 15 minutes, remove and serve.

This recipe makes enough for three or four people, and is best with thin toast and a salad of little romaine hearts tossed lightly in seasoned walnut oil and lime juice. A recent Dazaley [This is spelled Dézaley. And, of course, the alcoholic pattern of another's feast would not be as Swiss as I made mine in 1942. Each to his own nostalgia! In the 1950s . . . would it start this way: an oily Dutch gin with the smoked salmon . . . ?] at cellar temperature should be served amply with it, and with the coffee, strong and plentiful and preferably in café-glasses, you would undoubtedly have a *marc du Valais*, rather yellow and well able to jar your guests slightly where they sit.

The first sip would be polite. The second would be dogged. The rest would be good robust happiness, especially after the bland delicacy of the supper. The summer fireworks would start across the lake at Evian, and the baker boy who worked at night in Vevey would come hurtling down the road on his bicycle, yelling like a hilarious banshee as he took the curves of the corniche. The marc would make a warmth in you that might well last for several colder years.

Bœuf Moreno, like Eggs with Anchovies, or any other good recipe, needs no nostalgic introduction except the one you will always give it in your mind, after the first time you eat it. It is, like so many of the classics [. . . as well as in the undying perfection of the Laws of Moses] a hideous combination dietetically, and well worth trying.

Bœuf Moreno

2 *tablespoons butter*	2 *tablespoons chopped green*
2 *tablespoons flour*	*pepper or pimiento*
¾ *cup stock*	1 *pound leftover steak or roast*
4 *tablespoons mixed parsley*	*beef, 2 inches thick, cut in*
and chopped green onion or	*thin strips*
chives	½ *cup sour cream [I have now*
½ *cup mushrooms or pitted*	*increased this to one cup.]*
olives	3 *tablespoons brandy or*
2 *tablespoons butter*	*whiskey*
	hot rice or toast

Make a roux of the butter, flour, and stock. Add the onion and parsley, and simmer in a double boiler 20 minutes. Season.

Heat the peppers and mushrooms in 2 tablespoons butter in the bottom of a shallow casserole. Add the thin slices of beef and heat thoroughly.

Add the cream slowly to the roux, and stir in the brandy. Pour over the meat in the casserole. Serve at once, with hot fluffy rice or thin buttered toast.

A casserole that always makes me think of valentines, for no good reason, is made with young chicken and cream and is a fine way to ask, "Will you be my love?"

Poulet à la mode de Beaune

1 *tender chicken of about three pounds, cut in pieces*	*salt and fresh pepper and a little nutmeg*
½ *lemon*	1 *pint rich cream*
mixture of butter and olive oil [or chicken-fat from an earlier feast . . . and what is left makes a fine thing, once chilled, to eat upon good bread or toast.]	1 *dozen large mushrooms*
	3 *tablespoons butter*
	½ *cup fine brandy or marc*

Scrub the pieces of chicken thoroughly with the cut lemon. Dry, season, and fry thoroughly to a golden brown in the mixture of butter and oil.

Place the pieces in a casserole, and cover with the heated cream. Let cook in a moderate oven until tender.

Put butter in each mushroom cap, which has been washed quickly but not peeled, and cover the contents of the casserole with them. Broil quickly until done, about 5 minutes. Then quickly stir the mushrooms and the brandy into the casserole, and serve at once.

This is a rich and heady dish, as you can see. It needs a very cold and somewhat heavy white wine, like a Haut Sauternes. Or champagne will do nicely!

A refreshing delicate dessert that yet does not taste too sensible is indeed a rarity. Ices after heaviness are good, as the Italian cooks who first brought them to the French well knew, but they can seem overly thin. Fruit is the same, almost too natural and shocking after the high perverted flavors of some such masterpiece as Bœuf Moreno. But since a pudding or a soufflé would be unthinkable, why not serve thick slices of fresh pineapple soaked for several hours in an Alsatian *kirschwasser*, and then topped with a sherbet made with lime juice?

I ate this once in the richly muted dining room of a beautiful woman, and drank a dry champagne with it, and even if there had not been caviar in a big bowl long before, and little orchids like moths flying from a pink ruffled shell on the table, it would have been one of the perfect things of my gastronomic life.

The following recipe is very old, as age goes here. It was made often in Williamsburg, before there was any need of restoration, and undoubtedly pleased many a high-living Father of Our Country, both great and small.

Colonial Dessert

2 *cups thick cream*   1 *cup brown sugar*
4 *egg yolks*

Boil the cream one minute. Pour over the well-beaten egg yolks. Heat in a double boiler 8 minutes, beating constantly. Pour into a shallow dish from which it will be served, and chill overnight.

Two hours before serving cover with a half-inch layer of brown sugar, and brown very quickly under a hot broiler. Chill again, and serve with thin crisp cookies such as langues de chat.

A salad made of fruits, you could call the following eccentric dish. Paul Reboux, that antic gourmet, evolved it in his inimitable *cuisine au cerveau*, and called it, in the days when such things were slightly less impossible than now,

Fruits aux Sept Liqueurs

Put into an ample bowl the following: slices of orange, tangerines, and bananas; pitted cherries; wood strawberries and peeled grapes; sliced peeled peaches and plums and ripe pears. Sprinkle them with sugar and a little lime juice.

Pour over them the following liquid, which has been made of a wine-glassful each of the following but no other *liqueurs, all mixed thoroughly together: brandy, kirsch, Cointreau, Benedictine, maraschino, and a touch of kümmel.*

Stir the salad lightly, and put on ice for two hours. Just before serving, pour half a bottle of demi-sec *champagne over it.*

Yes, it is crazy, to sit savoring such impossibilities, while headlines yell at you and the wolf whuffs through the keyhole. Yet now and then it cannot harm you, thus to enjoy a short respite from reality. And if by chance you can indeed find some anchovies, or a thick slice of rare beef and some brandy, or a bowl of pink curled shrimps, you are doubly blessed, to possess in this troubled life both the capacity and the wherewithal to forget it for a time.

Conclusion

[This book came to its own conclusion several years ago, and upon rereading it I myself have reached a few more. But both the book and I agree, on one point made much further back than 1942, that since we must eat to live, we might as well do it with both grace and gusto.

Those few of us who actually live to eat are less repulsive than boring, and at this date I honestly know of only two such lost souls, gross puffy creatures, both of them, who are exhibited like any other monstrous curiosity by their well-fed but still balanced acquaintances.

On the other hand, I cannot count the good people I know who, to my mind, would be even better if they bent their spirits to the study of their own hungers. There are too many of us, otherwise in proper focus, who feel an impatience for the demands of our bodies, and who try throughout our whole lives, none too successfully, to deafen ourselves to the voices of our various hungers. Some stuff the wax of religious solace in our ears. Others practice a Spartan if somewhat pretentious disinterest in the pleasures of the flesh, or pretend that if we do not *admit our* sensual delight in a ripe nectarine we are not guilty . . . of even that tiny lust!

I believe that one of the most dignified ways we are capable of, to assert and then reassert our dignity in the face of poverty and war's fears and pains, is to nourish ourselves with all possible skill, delicacy, and ever-increasing enjoyment. And with our gastronomical growth will come, inevitably, knowledge and perception of a hundred other things, but mainly of ourselves. Then Fate, even tangled as it is with cold wars as well as hot, cannot harm us.]

Index of Recipes

Design by David Bullen
Typeset in Mergenthaler Bembo
by Wilsted & Taylor
Printed by Malloy Lithographing
on acid-free paper